# The Faith

# The Faith

Reflections on
the truths of the Apostles' Creed
from the teaching of

## POPE BENEDICT XVI

*Compiled and with an Introduction*
*by Paul Thigpen, Ph.D.*

Our Sunday Visitor Publishing Division
Our Sunday Visitor, Inc.
Huntington, Indiana 46750

18 17 16 15 14 13 1 2 3 4 5 6 7 8 9



ISBN 978-1-61278-667-4 (Inventory No. T1372)
eISBN: 978-1-61278-316-1
LCCN: 2013931519

Cover design by Lindsey Riesen

Cover art: *The Trinity*, St. Tretyakov Gallery, Moscow, Russia / The Bridgeman Art Library

PRINTED IN THE UNITED STATES OF AMERICA

# Contents

# Introduction

"Christian faith," Pope Benedict XVI has said, "is not only a matter of believing that certain things are true, but above all a personal relationship with Jesus Christ." In that succinct statement, he has given us an essential key to understanding all that he has taught about faith.

The Holy Father is a masterful theologian and biblical exegete. His scholarly work reflects a rare brilliance and beauty, delighting and challenging those who delve into the depths of his thought. But even a brief encounter with this work reveals clearly that his primary intention is not to engage in intriguing and elegant intellectual exercises. The scholarship always has a clear goal in mind: drawing his audience to Jesus Christ.

The same intention radiates from Pope Benedict's homilies and addresses to everyday Catholics. Their language is brief and simple, but they are nevertheless rich and deep. In these heartfelt words, he challenges the faithful to understand the Faith more fully so that they can know their Savior more deeply.

## *The Year of Faith*

We should not be surprised, then, that someone who has given his life to helping others know the Catholic faith would want to set aside an extended season for us all to ponder anew the meaning of our faith and to draw closer to Christ. In his Apostolic Letter *Porta Fidei* (October 11, 2011), Pope Benedict announced that the worldwide Church would observe a "Year of Faith" from October 11, 2012, to November 24, 2013. That announcement began with a stirring invitation and challenge:

"The 'door of faith' (Acts 14:27) is always open for us, ushering us into the life of communion with God and offering entry into His Church. It is possible to cross that threshold when the word of God is proclaimed and the heart allows itself to be shaped by transforming grace. To enter through that door is to set out on a journey that lasts a lifetime" (*Porta Fidei,* n. 1).

The Holy Father called on Catholics in all the parishes, religious communities, and other Catholic institutions around the world to find ways to observe this year through study, celebration, witness, and service. This book is one response to that call.

## *The Creed and the Sources*

What better place to begin with reflection on the Faith than with the Apostles' Creed? This ancient Christian statement of faith reflects the essentials of the apostolic tradition. It is embraced, not only by the Catholic Church, but by a number of other Christian communities as well. Each phrase of the creed crystallizes a central affirmation of our faith, worthy of careful meditation to draw out its meaning for our lives.

Who better to help us draw out that meaning than Pope Benedict himself? He has never published a commentary on the Apostles' Creed. But if he were to do so, no doubt it would reflect the themes and insights that are found already throughout his writing and preaching whenever he speaks about these essentials of Catholic faith. The plan of this book, then, is to identify those themes and present those insights as they can be gathered from the Holy Father's teaching since he was seated in St. Peter's Chair in 2005.

Although a few of the readings in this book come from magisterial documents or formal addresses to Church officials, most find their source in Pope Benedict's popular preaching. In that setting, his uncommon ability to present complex realities in simple, accessible terms has had ample room to shine.

Given that setting, many of the selections are homilies that take their cue from the great celebrations of the liturgical year. These observances are themselves intended to keep us mindful of the great truths of our faith: Advent and Christmas, Lent and Easter, solemnities of Our Lord and of Our Lady, and much more.

The Holy Father has also taken the opportunity to preach the great themes of faith in his weekly General Audience, when he addresses pilgrims gathered at St. Peter's Basilica in the Vatican. A number of the selections here come from that setting, where he offers concise spiritual reflections that warrant our careful study and application to everyday life.

In every setting, we encounter Pope Benedict's remarkable grasp of Sacred Scripture. Again and again, he takes us from the surface of its fertile soil down deep into its mysteries. There, faith finds a place to grow sturdy roots.

## *The Door of Faith Is Wide Open*

The resulting collection of readings, I trust, is a small sampling of a great harvest: the theological, biblical, and spiritual fruits that the Holy Father shares so generously with us all. In these pages we find food for the strenuous journey of faith — nourishing provisions from a wise and devoted Christian who profoundly understands our faith, who passionately loves "the pioneer and perfecter of our faith" (Heb 12:2), and who finds himself compelled to bring others to embrace the One who is worthy of our faith.

A note on the cover art: The famous icon *Trinity* by the medieval Russian artist Andrei Rublev (died c. 1430) depicts the three mysterious visitors who came to the Old Testament patriarch Abraham and were served a meal at the oak of Mamre (Gen 18:1–15). We are told that in the visit of these three figures, "the LORD appeared" to Abraham, and when the patriarch addressed them, he spoke to them in the singular, calling them "my lord." St. Augustine (354–430) and other ancient interpreters concluded that God was appearing to Abraham in the form of three Persons to signify the Blessed Trinity of Father, Son, and Holy Spirit.

The revelation of God's triune nature is at the heart of the Christian faith, the foundation for all the rest. So Rublev's icon seems a fitting choice for the cover.

In this Year of Faith, and in the years beyond, my hope is that this book will offer readers an occasion, as the Holy Father said, "when the word of God is proclaimed and the heart allows itself to be shaped by transforming grace."

The door of faith is wide open. Are you ready to set out on a journey that lasts a lifetime?

PAUL THIGPEN

---

**EDITOR'S NOTE:** With the exception of the Introduction by Paul Thigpen and the Apostles' Creed, the material in this book is derived from Pope Benedict XVI's audiences, speeches, encyclicals, letters, messages, and homilies. The texts have been edited only slightly to facilitate presentation in book form. The occasion and date of the original presentation is indicated at the end of each passeage.

# The Apostles' Creed

I believe in God,
the Father almighty,
Creator of heaven and earth,
and in Jesus Christ, His only Son, our Lord,
who was conceived by the Holy Spirit,
born of the Virgin Mary,
suffered under Pontius Pilate,
was crucified, died, and was buried;
He descended into hell;
on the third day He rose again from the dead;
He ascended into heaven,
and is seated at the right hand
  of God the Father almighty;
from there He will come to judge
  the living and the dead.
I believe in the Holy Spirit,
the holy catholic Church,
the communion of saints,
the forgiveness of sins,
the resurrection of the body,
and life everlasting. Amen.

CHAPTER ONE

# I Believe

## Faith, a Personal Relationship With Christ

Christian faith is not only a matter of believing that certain things are true, but above all a personal relationship with Jesus Christ. It is an encounter with the Son of God that gives new energy to the whole of our existence. When we enter into a personal relationship with Him, Christ reveals our true identity and, in friendship with Him, our life grows towards complete fulfillment....

Jesus said to Thomas: "Have you believed because you have seen Me? Blessed are those who have not seen and yet have come to believe" (Jn 20:29). He was thinking of the path the Church was to follow, based on the faith of eyewitnesses: the Apostles. Thus we come to see that our personal faith in Christ, which comes into being through dialogue with Him, is bound to the faith of the Church. We do not believe as isolated individuals, but rather, through Baptism, we are members of this great family; it is the faith professed by the Church which reinforces our personal faith.

The *Creed* that we proclaim at Sunday Mass protects us from the danger of believing in a God other than the one revealed by Christ: "Each believer is thus a link in the great chain of believers. I cannot believe without being carried by the faith of others, and by my faith I help support others in the faith" (*Catechism of the Catholic Church*, 166).

Let us always thank the Lord for the gift of the Church, for the Church helps us to advance securely in the faith that gives us true life (see Jn 20:31).

Message for World Youth Day, August 6, 2010

## Faith, Essential to Happiness

Let us listen once again to Elizabeth's words fulfilled in Mary's *Magnificat:* "Blessed is she who believed" (Lk 1:45). The first and fundamental act in order to become a dwelling place of God and thus find definitive happiness is to believe: It is faith, faith in God, in that God who showed himself in Jesus Christ and makes himself heard in the divine Word of Holy Scripture.

Believing is not adding one opinion to others. And the conviction, the belief, that God exists is not information like any other. Regarding most information, it makes no difference to us whether it is true or false; it does not change our lives. But if God does not exist, life is empty, the future is empty. And if God exists, everything changes, life is light, our future is light, and we have guidance for how to live.

Therefore, believing constitutes the fundamental orientation of our life. To believe, to say, "Yes, I believe that you are God, I believe that you are present among us in the Incarnate Son," gives my life a direction, impels me to be attached to God, to unite with God, and so to find my dwelling place, and the way to live.

To believe is not only a way of thinking or an idea … it is a way of acting, a manner of living. To believe means to follow the trail indicated to us by the Word of God.

Homily, Solemnity of the Assumption of the Blessed Virgin Mary, August 15, 2006

## Love, the Heart of Faith

"God is love, and he who abides in love abides in God, and God abides in him" (1 Jn 4:16). These words from the First Letter of John express with remarkable clarity the heart of the Christian faith: the Christian image of God and the resulting image of mankind and its destiny. In the same verse, St. John also offers a kind of summary of the Christian life: "We have come to know and to believe in the love God has for us."

*We have come to believe in God's love*: In these words the Christian can express the fundamental decision of his life. Being Christian is not the result of an ethical choice or a lofty idea, but the encounter with an event, a person, which gives life a new horizon and a decisive direction.

Encyclical Letter *Deus Caritas Est* (n. 1),
December 25, 2005

## Love, Born of Faith

Faith has a fundamental importance in the life of the Church, because the gift that God makes of Himself in Revelation is fundamental, and God's gift of himself is accepted through faith....

If ... the truth of the faith is placed simply and decisively at the heart of Christian existence, human life is innovated and revived by a love that knows no rest or bounds....

Charity, like love that renews all things, moves from God's Heart to the Heart of Jesus Christ, and through His Spirit across the world. This love is born from the encounter with Christ in faith.

Address to the Plenary Assembly for the Congregation for
the Doctrine of the Faith, February 5, 2006

## Faith, a Gift

Faith, understood as a fruit of the experience of God's love, is a grace, a gift of God. Yet human beings will only be able to experience faith as a grace to the extent that they accept it within themselves as a gift on which they seek to live.

For the 50th Anniversary of *Haurietis Aquas*, May 15, 2006

CHAPTER TWO

# In God, the Father Almighty

## God, the Source of Life

The desire for a more meaningful life is a sign that God created us and that we bear His "imprint." God is life, and that is why every creature reaches out towards life. Because human beings are made in the image of God, we do this in a unique and special way. We reach out for love, joy, and peace. So we can see how absurd it is to think that we can truly live by removing God from the picture!

God is the source of life. To set God aside is to separate ourselves from that source and, inevitably, to deprive ourselves of fulfillment and joy: "Without the Creator, the creature fades into nothingness" (Second Vatican Council, *Gaudium et Spes*, 36).

In some parts of the world, particularly in the West, today's culture tends to exclude God, and to consider faith a purely private issue with no relevance for the life of society. Even though the set of values underpinning society comes from the Gospel — values like the sense of the dignity of the person, of solidarity, of work, and of the family — we see a certain "eclipse of God" taking place, a kind of amnesia which, albeit not an outright rejection of Christianity, is nonetheless a denial of the treasure of our faith, a denial that could lead to the loss of our deepest identity.

For this reason, dear friends, I encourage you to strengthen your faith in God, the Father of our Lord Jesus Christ.

MESSAGE FOR WORLD YOUTH DAY, AUGUST 6, 2010

## God Is the True Father

Perhaps people today fail to perceive the beauty, greatness, and profound consolation contained in the word "father," with which we can turn to God in prayer, because today the father figure is often not sufficiently present and all too often is not sufficiently positive in daily life. The father's absence, the problem of a father who is not present in a child's life, is a serious problem of our time. It therefore becomes difficult to understand what it means to say that God is really our Father.

From Jesus Himself, from His filial relationship with God, we can learn what "father" really means and what is the true nature of the Father who is in heaven.

Critics of religion have said that speaking of the "Father," of God, is a projection of our ancestors in heaven. But the opposite is true: In the Gospel, Christ shows us who is the Father, and as He is a true father, we can understand true fatherhood and even learn true fatherhood.

Let us think of Jesus' words in the Sermon on the Mount, where He says: "But I say to you, love your enemies and pray for those who persecute you, so that you may be sons of your Father who is in heaven" (Mt 5:44–45). It is the very love of Jesus, the Only-Begotten Son — who goes even to the point of giving himself on the Cross — that reveals to us the true nature of the Father: He is Love, and in our prayers as children we too enter this circuit of love, the love of God that purifies our desires, our attitudes marked by closure, self-sufficiency, and the typical selfishness of the former man.

We could therefore say that … God is our Father because He is our Creator. Each one of us, each man and each woman, is a miracle of God, is wanted by Him, and is personally known by Him. When it says in the Book of Genesis that the human being is created in the image of God (see Gen 1:27), it tries to express this precise reality: God is our Father; for Him we are not anonymous, impersonal beings, but have a name.

General Audience, May 23, 2012

## The Spirit Teaches Us to Call God "Father"

The Holy Spirit [is] the great master of prayer who teaches us to address God with the affectionate words that children use, calling him, "Abba, Father." This is what Jesus did.

Even in the most dramatic moment of His earthly life, He never lost His trust in the Father and always called on Him with the intimacy of the beloved Son. In Gethsemane, when He feels the anguish of His approaching death, His prayer is "Abba, Father, all things are possible to you; remove this cup from me; yet not what I will, but what you will" (Mk 14:36).

Since the very first steps on her journey the Church has taken up this invocation and made it her own, especially in the prayer of the "Our Father," in which we say every day: "Our Father … Thy will be done, on earth as it is in heaven!" (Mt 6:9–10).

We find it twice in the Letters of St. Paul. The Apostle … addresses these words to the Galatians: "And because you are sons, God has sent the Spirit of His Son into our hearts, crying, 'Abba! Father!'" (Gal 4:6).

And at the center of that hymn to the Holy Spirit which is the eighth chapter of the Letter to the Romans, St. Paul declares: "For you did not receive the spirit of slavery to fall back into fear, but you have received the spirit of sonship. When we cry: 'Abba! Father!' it is the Spirit himself..." (Rom 8:15).

General Audience, May 23, 2012

## The Spirit Makes Us Children of God

Christianity is not a religion of fear, but of trust and of love for the Father who loves us. Both these crucial affirmations speak to us of the sending forth and reception of the Holy Spirit, the gift of the risen One which makes us sons in Christ, the Only-Begotten Son, and places us in a filial relationship with God, a relationship of deep trust, like that of children; a filial relationship like that of Jesus, even though its origin and quality are different.

Jesus is the eternal Son of God who took flesh. We instead become sons in Him, in time, through faith, and through the sacraments of Baptism and Confirmation. Thanks to these two sacraments we are immersed in the paschal mystery of Christ.

The Holy Spirit is the precious and necessary gift that makes us children of God, that brings about that adoption as sons to which all human beings are called because, as the divine blessing in the Letter to the Ephesians explains, God, in Christ, "chose us in Him before the foundation of the world, that we should be holy and blameless before Him. He destined us in love to be His [adopted] sons through Jesus Christ" (Eph 1:4)....

St. Paul's two passages on this action of the Holy Spirit ... correspond with each other but contain a different nuance. In the Letter to the Galatians ... the Apostle says that the Spirit cries, "Abba! Father!" in us. In the Letter to the Romans he says that it is we who cry, "Abba! Father!"...

St. Paul wants to make us understand that Christian prayer is never one way, never happens in one direction from us to God. It is never merely "an action of ours," but rather is the expression of a reciprocal relationship in which God is the first to act. It is the Holy Spirit who cries in us, and we are able to cry because the impetus comes from the Holy Spirit.

We would not be able to pray were the desire for God, for being children of God, not engraved in the depths of our heart. Since he came into existence, *homo sapiens* has always been in search of God and endeavors to speak with God because God has engraved himself in our hearts.

The first initiative therefore comes from God, and with Baptism, once again God acts in us, the Holy Spirit acts in us. He is the prime initiator of prayer so that we may really converse with God and say "Abba" to God. Hence His presence opens our prayers and our lives; it opens on to the horizons of the Trinity and of the Church.

General Audience, May 23, 2012

## Two Dimensions of God's Fatherhood

A phrase in the Psalms always moves me when I pray: "Your hands have made and fashioned me," says the psalmist (Ps 119:73). In this beautiful image each one of us can express his personal relationship with God. "Your hands have fashioned me. You thought of me and created and wanted me."

Nonetheless, this is still not enough. The Spirit of Christ opens us to a second dimension of God's fatherhood, beyond creation, since Jesus is the "Son" in the full sense of "one in being with the Father," as we profess in the Creed. Becoming a human being like us, with His incarnation, death, and resurrection, Jesus in His turn accepts us in His humanity and even in His being Son, so that we too may enter into His specific belonging to God.

Of course, our being children of God does not have the fullness of Jesus. We must increasingly become so throughout the journey of our Christian existence, developing in the following of Christ and in communion with Him so as to enter ever more intimately into the relationship of love with God the Father which sustains our life.

It is this fundamental reality that is disclosed to us when we open ourselves to the Holy Spirit and He makes us turn to God saying "Abba," Father. We have truly preceded creation, entering into adoption with Jesus; united, we are really in God and are His children in a new way, in a new dimension.

General Audience, May 23, 2012

## Many Children of One Father

The prayer of the Spirit of Christ in us and ours in Him is not solely an individual act, but an act of the entire Church. In praying, our heart is opened. Not only do we enter into communion with God, but actually with all the children of God, because we are one body. When we address the Father in our inner room in silence and in recollection, we are never alone.

Those who speak to God are not alone. We are within the great prayer of the Church. We are part of a great symphony that the Christian community, in all the parts of the earth and in all epochs, raises to God. Naturally, the musicians and instruments differ — and this is an element of enrichment — but the melody of praise is one and in harmony.

Every time, then, that we shout or say, "Abba! Father!" it is the Church, the whole communion of people in prayer, that supports our invocation; and our invocation is an invocation of the Church.

This is also reflected in the wealth of charisms and of the ministries and tasks that we carry out in the community. St. Paul writes to the Christians of Corinth: "There are varieties of gifts, but the same Spirit; and there are varieties of service, but the same Lord; and there are varieties of working, but it is the same God who inspires them all in everyone" (1 Cor 12:4–6).

Prayer guided by the Holy Spirit, who makes us say, "Abba! Father!" with Christ and in Christ, inserts us into the great mosaic of the family of God, in which each one has a place and an important role, in profound unity with the whole.…

We also learn to cry "Abba! Father!" with Mary, Mother of the Son of God. The consummation of the fullness of time, of which St. Paul speaks in his Letter to the Galatians (see Gal 4:4), is brought about at the moment when Mary said "yes," the moment of her full adherence to God's will: "Behold, I am the handmaid of the Lord" (Lk 1:38).

Dear brothers and sisters, let us learn to savor in our prayers the beauty of being friends, indeed children of God, of being able to call on Him with the trust that a child has for the parents who love him. Let us open our prayers to the action of the Holy Spirit so that He may cry to God in us,

"Abba! Father!" and so that our prayers may transform and constantly convert our way of thinking and our action to bring us ever more closely into line with Jesus Christ, the Only-Begotten Son of God.

General Audience, May 23, 2012

CHAPTER THREE

# Creator of Heaven and Earth

## Salvation History Begins with Creation

At the Easter Vigil, the journey along the paths of Sacred Scripture begins with the account of creation. This is the liturgy's way of telling us that the creation story is itself a prophecy. It is not information about the external processes by which the cosmos and man himself came into being.

The Fathers of the Church were well aware of this. They did not interpret the story as an account of the process of the origins of things, but rather as a pointer towards the essential, towards the true beginning and end of our being.

Now one might ask: Is it really important to speak also of creation during the Easter Vigil? Could we not begin with the events in which God calls man, forms a people for himself, and creates His history with men upon the earth? The answer must be no. To omit the creation would be to misunderstand the very history of God with men, to diminish it, to lose sight of its true order of greatness.

The sweep of history established by God reaches back to the origins, back to creation. Our profession of faith begins with the words: "We believe in God, the Father Almighty, Creator of heaven and earth." If we omit the beginning of the *Credo*, the whole history of salvation becomes too limited and too small.

The Church is not some kind of association that concerns itself with man's religious needs but is limited to that objective. No, she brings man into contact with God and thus with the Source of all things. Therefore we relate to God as Creator, and so we have a responsibility for creation.

Our responsibility extends as far as creation because it comes from the Creator. Only because God created everything can He give us life and direct our lives. Life in the Church's faith involves more than a set of feelings and sentiments and perhaps moral obligations. It embraces man in his entirety, from his origins to his eternal destiny.

Only because creation belongs to God can we place ourselves completely in His hands. And only because He is the Creator can He give us life for ever. Joy over creation, thanksgiving for creation, and responsibility for it all belong together.

HOMILY, EASTER VIGIL, APRIL 23, 2011

## ALL THINGS CREATED THROUGH THE WORD

The central message of the creation account [in the Book of Genesis] can be defined more precisely still. In the opening words of his Gospel, St. John sums up the essential meaning of that account in this single statement: "In the beginning was the Word" (Jn 1:1).

In effect, the creation account [in Genesis] … is characterized by the regularly recurring phrase: "And God said …" The world is a product of the Word, of the *Logos*, as St. John expresses it, using a key term from the Greek language.

"*Logos*" means "reason," "sense," "word." It is not reason pure and simple, but creative Reason, which speaks and communicates itself. It is Reason that both is and creates sense. The creation account tells us, then, that the world is a product of creative Reason.

Hence it tells us that, far from there being an absence of reason and freedom at the origin of all things, the source of everything is creative Reason, love, and freedom. Here we are faced with the ultimate alternative that is at stake in the dispute between faith and unbelief: Are irrationality, lack of freedom, and pure chance the origin of everything? Or are reason, freedom, and love at the origin of being? Does the primacy belong to unreason or to reason?

This is what everything hinges upon in the final analysis. As believers we answer, with the creation account and with John, that in the beginning is reason.

In the beginning is freedom. Hence it is good to be a human person. It is not the case that in the expanding universe, at a late stage, in some tiny corner of the cosmos, there evolved randomly some species of living being capable of reasoning and of trying to find rationality within creation, or to bring rationality into it. If man were merely a random product of evolution in some place on the margins of the universe, then his life would make no sense or might even be a chance of nature.

But no, Reason is there at the beginning: creative, divine Reason. And because it is Reason, it also created freedom; and because freedom can be abused, there also exist forces harmful to creation. Hence a thick black line, so to speak, has been drawn across the structure of the universe and across the nature of man.

But despite this contradiction, creation itself remains good, life remains good, because at the beginning is good Reason, God's creative love. Hence the world can be saved. Hence we can and must place ourselves on the side of reason, freedom and love — on the side of God who loves us so much that He suffered for us, that from His death there might emerge a new, definitive, and healed life.

HOMILY, EASTER VIGIL, APRIL 23, 2011

## CREATION, SABBATH, AND COVENANT

The Old Testament account of creation ... has structured the process of creation within the framework of a week leading up to the Sabbath, in which it finds its completion. For Israel, the Sabbath was the day on which all could participate in God's rest, in which man and animal, master and slave, great and small were united in God's freedom. Thus the Sabbath was an expression of the covenant between God and man and creation.

In this way, communion between God and man does not appear as something extra, something added later to a world already fully created. The covenant, communion between God and man, is inbuilt at the deepest level of creation.

Yes, the covenant is the inner ground of creation, just as creation is the external presupposition of the covenant. God made the world so that there could be a space where He might communicate His love, and from which the response of love might come back to Him. From God's perspective, the heart of the man who responds to Him is greater and more important than the whole immense material cosmos, for all that the latter allows us to glimpse is something of God's grandeur.

HOMILY, EASTER VIGIL, APRIL 23, 2011

## The Cosmos Reflects the Creator Spirit

Words found at the beginning of the Creation account … speak of the Creator Spirit who sweeps over the face of the abyss, who creates the world and renews it constantly. Faith in the Creator Spirit is an essential part of the Christian creed. The fact that matter has a mathematical structure, is spirit-filled, is the basis of the modern natural sciences.

It is only because matter is structured intelligently that our mind can interpret and actively refashion it. The fact that this intelligible structure comes from the same Creator Spirit who also gave us our own spirit, brings with it both a duty and a responsibility.

Our faith in creation is the ultimate basis of our responsibility for the earth. The earth is not simply our property, which we can exploit according to our interests and desires. Rather, it is a gift of the Creator, who designed its innate order and has thus given us guidelines which we, as stewards of His creation, need to respect. The fact that the earth and the cosmos mirror the Creator Spirit also means that their rational structures which, beyond their mathematical order, become almost tangible in scientific experimentation, also have an inherent ethical orientation.

The Spirit who fashioned them is more than mathematics — He is Goodness in person who, in and through the language of creation, points out to us the way of an upright life.

Since faith in the Creator is an essential part of the Christian creed, the Church cannot and must not limit herself to passing on to the faithful the message of salvation alone. She has a responsibility towards creation, and must also publicly assert this responsibility. In so doing, she must not only defend earth, water, and air as gifts of creation belonging to all. She must also protect man from self-destruction. What is needed is something like a human ecology, correctly understood....

An integral part of the Church proclamation must be a witness to the Creator Spirit present in nature as a whole, and, in a special way, in the human person, created in God's image.

Address to the Roman Curia, December 22, 2008

CHAPTER FOUR

# And in Jesus Christ

## Christ Himself Is Truth

Jesus Christ is the personified Truth who attracts the world to himself. The light that shines out from Jesus is the splendor of the truth. Every other truth is a fragment of the Truth that He is, and refers to Him.

Jesus is the Pole Star of human freedom: Without Him it loses its sense of direction, for without the knowledge of truth, freedom degenerates, becomes isolated and is reduced to sterile arbitration. With Him, freedom is rediscovered; it is recognized to have been created for our good and is expressed in charitable actions and behavior.

Therefore, Jesus gives men and women total familiarity with the truth and continuously invites them to live in it. It is truth offered as a reality that restores the human being and at the same time surpasses him and towers above him, as a Mystery that embraces and at the same time exceeds the impulse of his intelligence.

And nothing succeeds as well as love for the truth in impelling the human mind towards unexplored horizons. Jesus Christ, who is the fullness of the truth, draws to himself the heart of each person, enlarges it and fills it with joy. Indeed, truth alone can take possession of the mind and make it rejoice to the full.

It is this joy that increases the dimensions of the human heart, lifting it anew from the narrowness of selfishness and rendering it capable of authentic love. It is the experience of this joy that moves and attracts the human person to free adoration — not to servile prostration, but to bow with heartfelt respect before the Truth he has encountered.

Thus, service to the faith, which is a witness to the One who is the entire Truth, is also a service to joy, and this is the joy that Christ desires to spread in the world: It is the joy of faith in Him, of truth that is communicated through Him, of salvation that comes from Him! It is this joy we feel in our hearts when we kneel with faith to worship Jesus!

ADDRESS TO THE PLENARY ASSEMBLY FOR THE CONGREGATION FOR THE DOCTRINE OF THE FAITH, FEBRUARY 5, 2006

## CHRIST SHOWS US GOD'S LOVE

"Having loved His own who were in the world, He loved them to the end" (Jn 13:1).

God loves His creature, man: He even loves him in his fall and does not leave him to himself. He loves him to the end. He is impelled with His love to the very end, to the extreme: He came down from His divine glory.

He cast aside the raiment of His divine glory and put on the garb of a slave. He came down to the extreme lowliness of our fall. He kneels before us and carries out for us the service of a slave: He washes our dirty feet so that we might be admitted to God's banquet and be made worthy to take our place at His table — something that on our own we neither could nor would ever be able to do.

God is not a remote God, too distant or too great to be bothered with our trifles. Since God is great, He can also be concerned with small things. Since He is great, the soul of man, the same man, created through eternal love, is not a small thing, but great, and worthy of God's love.

God's holiness is not merely an incandescent power before which we are obliged to withdraw, terrified. It is a power of love and therefore a purifying and healing power.

God descends and becomes a slave; He washes our feet so that we may come to His table. In this, the entire mystery of Jesus Christ is expressed. In this, what redemption means becomes visible.

The basin in which He washes us is His love, ready to face death. Only love has that purifying power which washes the grime from us and elevates us to God's heights.

The basin that purifies us is God himself, who gives himself to us without reserve — to the very depths of His suffering and His death. He is ceaselessly this love that cleanses us; in the sacraments of purification — Baptism and the Sacrament of Penance — He is continually on His knees at our feet and carries out for us the service of a slave, the service of purification, making us capable of God.

His love is inexhaustible; it truly goes to the very end.

HOMILY, MASS OF THE LORD'S SUPPER, APRIL 13, 2006

## FAITH IN JESUS

I would like briefly to reflect on the Gospel … text in which we find the celebrated dictum *"Nemo propheta in patria,"* that is, no prophet is gladly accepted among his own people, who had watched him grow up (see Mk 6:4). In effect, after Jesus left Nazareth at about [the age of] 30 years, and had already for some time been preaching and healing elsewhere, He returned to His town and began to teach in the synagogue. His fellow townsmen "were stupefied" by His wisdom and, knowing Him as "Mary's son," the "carpenter" who had lived with them, instead of welcoming Him with faith they were scandalized by him (see Mk 6:2–3).

This is an understandable reaction, since familiarity on a human level makes it hard to go farther and open up to the divine dimension. It is difficult for them to believe that this carpenter would be the Son of God. Jesus himself brings up the example of the prophets of Israel, who in their own country were objects of scorn, and He identifies with them.

Because of this spiritual closedness, in Nazareth Jesus was "not able to perform any mighty deed there, apart from curing a few sick people by laying His hands on them" (Mk 6:5). In fact, Christ's miracles are not exhibitions of power but signs of God's love, which actualizes itself where it meets man's faith. It is a reciprocity. Origen writes: "In the same way that some bodies are attracted to each other, as the magnet to iron … so also faith exerts an attraction on divine power" (*Commentary on Matthew's Gospel,* 10, 19).

It seems, therefore, that Jesus is able to have some success in Nazareth despite the poor reception He receives. However, at the end of the account, we find an observation that states the contrary. The evangelist writes that Jesus "marveled at their lack of faith" (Mk 6:6).

Jesus' surprise corresponds to the stupor of His fellow townsmen, who are scandalized. Even Jesus is in a certain sense scandalized! Although He knows that no prophet is gladly accepted in his homeland, He regards the closure of His people's hearts as strange, inscrutable: How is it possible that they do not recognize the light of Truth? Why do they not open themselves to the goodness of God who wanted to share our humanity?

In effect, the man Jesus of Nazareth is the transparency of God; in Him, God lives fully. And [as long as] we too always seek other signs, other mighty deeds, we do not see that He is the true Lord, God made flesh; He is the greatest miracle of the universe: all of God's love enclosed within a human Heart, in the countenance of a Man.

The Virgin Mary is she who truly understood this reality, blessed because she believed (see Lk 1:45). Mary is not scandalized by her Son: Her wonder over Him is full of faith, full of love and joy, in seeing Him at the same time so human and so divine. Let us therefore learn from her, our Mother in the faith, to recognize the perfect revelation of God in the humanity of Christ.

Angelus Homily, July 8, 2012

## Open Wide the Doors to Christ!

If we let Christ into our lives, we lose nothing, nothing, absolutely nothing of what makes life free, beautiful, and great. No! Only in this friendship are the doors of life opened wide. Only in this friendship is the great potential of human existence truly revealed. Only in this friendship do we experience beauty and liberation.

And so, today, with great strength and great conviction, on the basis of long personal experience of life, I say to you, dear young people: Do not be afraid of Christ! He takes nothing away, and He gives you everything. When we give ourselves to Him, we receive a hundredfold in return. Yes, open, open wide the doors to Christ — and you will find true life.

Homily, Papal Installation Mass, April 24, 2005

CHAPTER FIVE

# His Only Son

## Jesus Is More Than a Prophet

The people thought that Jesus was a prophet. This was not wrong, but it does not suffice; it is inadequate. In fact, it was a matter of delving deep, of recognizing the uniqueness of the person of Jesus of Nazareth and His newness.

This is how it still is today: Many people draw near to Jesus, as it were, from the outside. Great scholars recognize His spiritual and moral stature and His influence on human history, comparing him to Buddha, Confucius, Socrates, and other wise and important historical figures.

Yet they do not manage to recognize Him in His uniqueness. What Jesus said to Philip at the Last Supper springs to mind: "Have I been with you so long, and yet you do not know me, Philip?" (Jn 14:9).

Jesus is often also considered as one of the great founders of a religion from which everyone may take something in order to form his or her own conviction. Today too, people have different opinions about Jesus, just as they did then. And as He did then, Jesus also repeats His question to us, His disciples today: "And who do you say that I am?" (Mk 8:29; Lk 9:20; Mt 16:15).

Let us make Peter's answer our own. According to the Gospel of Mark, he said: "You are the Christ" (8:29); in Luke, the affirmation is "the Christ of God" (Lk 9:20); in Matthew resounds, "You are the Christ, the Son of the living God" (16:16); finally, in John: "You are the Holy One of

God" (Jn 6:69). These are all correct answers which are also right for us.

HOMILY, SOLEMNITY OF SAINTS PETER AND PAUL, JUNE 29, 2007

## JESUS IS GOD HIMSELF MADE MAN

What was it that the people to whom Jesus was speaking found hard to accept? What continues to be hard for many people also in our time?

It is difficult to accept that He claimed not only to be one of the prophets but the Son of God, and that He claimed God's own authority for himself.

Listening to Him preaching, seeing Him heal the sick, evangelize the lowly and the poor, and reconcile sinners, little by little the disciples came to realize that He was the Messiah in the most exalted sense of the word; that is, not only a man sent by God, but God himself made Man.

Clearly, all this was far beyond them; it exceeded their capacity for understanding. They were able to express their faith with the titles of the Judaic tradition: "Christ," "Son of God," "Lord." However, to adhere truly to reality, these titles had in some way to be rediscovered in their most profound truth: Jesus himself revealed their true meaning with His life, ever surprising, even paradoxical, considering the customary concepts.

And the faith of the disciples itself had to adapt progressively. It presents itself as a pilgrimage which begins in the experience of the historical Jesus, finds its foundation in the Paschal Mystery, but must then advance further thanks to the working of the Holy Spirit.

This was also the faith of the Church in the course of history; this is also our faith as Christians of today. Firmly resting on the "rock" of Peter, it is a pilgrimage toward the fullness of that truth which the Fisherman of Galilee professed with passionate conviction: "You are the Christ, the Son of the Living God" (Mt 16:16).

HOMILY, SOLEMNITY OF SAINTS PETER AND PAUL, JUNE 29, 2007

## THE MYSTERY OF CHRIST'S SONSHIP

When Jesus was twelve years old … He went with His parents to the temple of Jerusalem.… [Here are] the first words of Jesus … recorded: "How is it that you sought Me? Did you not know that I must be in my Father's house?" (Lk 2:49).

After three days spent looking for Him, His parents found Him in the temple, sitting among the teachers, listening to them and asking them questions (see 2:46). His answer to the question of why He had done this to His father and mother was that He had only done what the Son should do, that is, to be with His Father.

Thus He showed who is the true Father, what is the true home, and that He had done nothing unusual or disobedient. He had stayed where the Son ought to be, that is, with the Father, and He stressed who His Father was.

The term "Father" therefore dominates the tone of this answer and the Christological mystery appears in its entirety. Hence, this word unlocks the mystery. It is the key to the mystery of Christ, who is the Son, and also the key to our mystery as Christians who are sons and daughters in the Son.

At the same time Jesus teaches us to be children by being with the Father in prayer. The Christological mystery, the mystery of Christian existence, is closely linked to, founded on, prayer.

Jesus was one day to teach His disciples to pray, telling them: When you pray, say, "Father." And, naturally, do not just say the word; say it with your life, learn to say it meaningfully with your life: "Father." And in this way you will be true sons in the Son, true Christians.

It is important at this point, when Jesus was still fully integrated in the life of the Family of Nazareth, to note the resonance that hearing this word "Father" on Jesus' lips must have had in the hearts of Mary and Joseph. It is also important to reveal, to emphasize, who the Father is, and, with His awareness, to hear this word on the lips of the Only-Begotten Son who, for this very reason, chose to stay on for three days in the Temple, which is the "Father's house."

We may imagine that from this time the life of the Holy Family must have been even more full of prayer, since from the heart of Jesus the boy — then an adolescent and a young man — this deep meaning of the relationship with God the Father would not cease to spread and to be echoed in the hearts of Mary and Joseph.

This episode shows us the real situation, the atmosphere, of being with the Father. So it was that the Family of Nazareth became the first model of the Church in which, around the presence of Jesus and through His mediation, everyone experiences the filial relationship with God the Father which also transforms interpersonal human relationships.

General Audience, December 28, 2011

## Jesus and His Father in Prayer

"I give praise to You, Father, Lord of heaven and earth …" (Mt 11:25).

The Evangelists Matthew and Luke (see Mt 11:25–30; Lk 10:21–22) have handed down to us a "jewel" of Jesus' prayer that is often called the Cry of Exultation.… It is a prayer of thanksgiving and praise.…

In the original Greek of the Gospels the word with which this jubilation begins, and which expresses Jesus' attitude in addressing the Father, is … often translated with the word … "praise" (cf. Mt 11:25 and Lk 10:21). However, in the New Testament writings this term indicates mainly two things: The first is "to confess" fully…; the second thing is "to be in agreement."

Therefore, the words with which Jesus begins His prayer contain His full recognition of the Father's action and at the same time, His being in total, conscious, and joyful agreement with this way of acting, with the Father's plan. The "Cry of Exultation" is the apex of a journey of prayer in which Jesus' profound and close communion with the life of the Father in the Holy Spirit clearly emerges, and His divine Sonship is revealed.

Jesus addresses God by calling him "Father." This word expresses Jesus' awareness and certainty of being "the Son" in intimate and constant communion with Him, and this is the central focus and source of every one of Jesus' prayers. We see it clearly in the last part of the hymn, which illuminates the entire text.

Jesus said: "All things have been delivered to me by my Father; and no one knows who the Son is except the Father, or who the Father is except the Son and any one to whom the Son chooses to reveal Him" (Lk 10:22). Jesus was therefore affirming that only "the Son" truly knows the Father.

All the knowledge that people have of each other — we all experience this in our human relationships — entails involvement, a certain inner bond between the one who knows and the one who is known, at a more or less profound level: We cannot know anyone without a communion of being. In the Cry of Exultation — as in all His prayers — Jesus shows that true knowledge of God presupposes communion with Him. Only by being in communion with the other can I begin to know him; and so it is with God: Only if I am in true contact, if I am in communion with Him, can I also know Him.

True knowledge, therefore, is reserved to the "Son," the Only Begotten One who is in the bosom of the Father since eternity (see Jn 1:18), in perfect unity with Him. The Son alone truly knows God, since He is in an intimate communion of being; only the Son can truly reveal who God is....

Luke the Evangelist introduces the prayer with the annotation: Jesus "rejoiced in the Holy Spirit" (Lk 10:21). Jesus rejoiced from the depths of His being, in what counted most: His unique communion of knowledge and love with the Father, the fullness of the Holy Spirit. By involving us in His Sonship, Jesus invites us too to open ourselves to the light of the Holy Spirit, since — as the Apostle Paul affirms — "we do not know how to pray as we ought, but the Spirit himself intercedes for us with sighs too deep for words ... according to the will of God" (Rom 8:26–27), and reveals the Father's love to us.

In Matthew's Gospel, following the Cry of Exultation, we find one of Jesus' most heartfelt appeals: "Come to me, all who labor and are heavy laden, and I will give you rest" (Mt 11:28). Jesus asks us to go to Him, for He is true Wisdom; to Him who is "gentle and lowly in heart." He offers us His "yoke," the way of the wisdom of the Gospel, which is neither a doctrine to be learned nor an ethical system, but rather a Person to follow: He himself, the Only-Begotten Son in perfect communion with the Father.

General Audience, December 7, 2011

## "Abba"

Another element of this prayer [of Jesus in Gethsemane] seems to me to be important. The three witnesses preserved — as appears in Sacred Scripture — the Hebrew or Aramaic word with which the Lord spoke to the Father. He called him: *Abba,* "Father."

But this term *Abba* is a familiar form of the term "father," a form used only in the family that was never applied to God. Here we have a glimpse of Jesus' intimate life, of the way He spoke in the family, the way He truly spoke as the Son with the Father. We see the Trinitarian mystery: The Son speaks to the Father and redeems humanity.

General Audience, April 20, 2011

CHAPTER SIX

# Our Lord

## "Jesus Is Lord"

The Holy Spirit is the One who makes us recognize the Lord in Christ and prompts us to speak the profession of the Church's faith: "Jesus is Lord" (1 Cor 12:3b). "Lord" is the title attributed to God in the Old Testament, a title that in the interpretation of the Bible replaced His unpronounceable name.

The Creed of the Church is nothing other than the development of what we say with this simple affirmation: "Jesus is Lord." Concerning this profession of faith, St. Paul tells us that it is precisely a matter of the word and work of the Spirit. If we want to be in the Spirit, we must adhere to this Creed. By making it our own, by accepting it as our word, we gain access to the work of the Holy Spirit.

The words "Jesus is Lord" can be interpreted in two ways. They mean: Jesus is God and, at the same time, God is Jesus. The Holy Spirit illuminates this reciprocity: Jesus has divine dignity, and God has the human face of Jesus. God shows himself in Jesus, and by doing so gives us the truth about ourselves.

Homily, Pentecost, June 12, 2011

## Jesus, the Only Lord

The hymn in the *Letter to the Philippians* [see Phil 2:5–11] offers us important instructions for our prayers. The first is in the invocation "Lord," addressed to Jesus Christ, seated at the right hand of the Father: He is the one Lord of our life, among so many "dominant" people who desire to direct and guide it.

For this reason, it is necessary to have a scale of values in which the primacy is God's, in order to affirm with St. Paul: "I count everything as loss because of the surpassing worth of knowing Christ Jesus my Lord" (Phil 3:8). The encountering with the risen One made the Apostle realize that He is the one treasure for which it is worth expending one's life.

The second instruction is prostration, that "every knee shall bow," on earth and in heaven. This is reminiscent of words of the Prophet Isaiah, where he points to the worship that all creatures owe to God (see Is 45:23). Genuflection or kneeling in prayer before the Blessed Sacrament exactly expresses the attitude of adoration in God's presence and also with the body. Hence the importance of not doing this action out of habit or hastily, but rather with profound awareness. When we kneel before the Lord, we profess our faith in Him, we acknowledge that He is the one Lord of our life.

Dear brothers and sisters, in our prayers let us fix our gaze on the crucified One; let us pause more often in adoration before the Eucharist to let our life enter the love of God, who humbly lowered himself in order to lift us up to Him.

General Audience, June 27, 2012

## Jesus, Lord and King

In the New Testament, Peter becomes the "rock" of the Church insofar as He is the bearer of Faith: The "we" of the Church begins with the name of the first man who professed faith in Christ. It begins with *his* faith, a faith that was at first immature and still "too human."

Then, however, after Easter it matured and made him capable of following Christ even to the point of giving himself. It developed in the belief that Jesus is truly King; that He is so precisely because He *remained* on the Cross, and *in that way* gave His life for sinners.

In the Gospel we see that everyone asks Jesus to come down from the Cross. They mock Him, but this is also a way of excusing themselves from blame, as if to say:

"It is not our fault that You are hanging on the Cross; it is solely Your fault, because if You really were the Son of God, the King of the Jews, You would not stay there but would save Yourself by coming down from that infamous scaffold. Therefore, if you remain there, it means that You are wrong and we are right."

The tragedy that is played out beneath the cross of Jesus is a universal tragedy. It concerns all people before God, who reveals himself for what He is, namely, Love.

In the crucified Jesus the divinity is disfigured, stripped of all visible glory, and yet it is present and real. Faith alone can recognize it: the faith of Mary, who places in her heart too this last scene in the mosaic of her Son's life. She does not yet see the whole, but continues to trust in God, repeating once again with the same abandonment: "Behold, the handmaid of the Lord" (see Lk 1:38).

Then there is the faith of the Good Thief: a faith barely outlined but sufficient to assure him salvation: "Today you will be with me in Paradise." This "with me" is crucial.

Yes, it is this that saves him.

Of course, the Good Thief is on the cross *like* Jesus, but above all he is on the Cross *with* Jesus. And, unlike the other evildoer and all those who taunt him, he does not ask Jesus to come done from the Cross nor to make him come down.

Instead he says: "Remember me when You come into Your kingdom."

The Good Thief sees Jesus on the Cross, disfigured and unrecognizable, and yet he entrusts himself to Him as to a king, indeed as to *the* King. The Good Thief believes what was written on the tablet over Jesus' head: "The King of the Jews." He believed and entrusted himself. For this reason he was already, immediately, in the "today" of God, in Paradise, because Paradise is this: being *with* Jesus, being *with* God.

So here, dear brothers, is the first and fundamental message that the word of God clearly tells us today: ... It calls us to *be with* Jesus, like Mary, and not to ask Him to come down from the Cross, but rather to stay there with Him. And by reason of our ministry we must do this not only for ourselves but for the whole Church, for the whole People of God.

HOMILY, SOLEMNITY OF CHRIST THE KING, NOVEMBER 21, 2010

## PARTICIPATING IN THE LORDSHIP OF CHRIST

We know from the Gospels that the Cross was the critical point of the faith of Simon Peter and of the other Apostles. It is clear and it could not be otherwise: They were men and thought "according to men"; they could not tolerate the idea of a crucified Messiah.

Peter's "conversion" is fully achieved when he stops wanting to "save" Jesus and accepts to be saved by Him. He gives up wanting to save Jesus from the Cross and allows Jesus' cross to save him.

"I have prayed for you that your faith may not fail; and when you have turned again, strengthen your brethren" (Lk 22:32), the Lord says. Peter's ministry consists first of all in his faith, a faith that Jesus immediately recognizes, from the outset, as genuine, as a gift of the heavenly Father. But [it is] a faith that must pass through the scandal of the Cross to become authentic, truly "Christian," to become a "rock" on which Jesus can build his Church.

Participation in the lordship of Christ is only brought about in practice in the sharing of His self-abasement, with the Cross. My ministry too, dear brothers, and consequently also yours, consists wholly of faith. Jesus can build His Church on us as long as that true Paschal faith is found in us, that faith which does not seek to make Jesus come down from the Cross but entrusts itself to Him on the Cross. In this regard, the true place of the Vicar of Christ is the Cross; it lies in persisting in the obedience of the Cross.

This ministry is difficult because it is not in line with the human way of thinking — with that natural logic which, moreover, continues to be active within us too. But this is and always remains our primary service, the service of faith that transforms the whole of life: believing that Jesus is God, that He is the King precisely *because* He reached that point, because He loved us to the very end.

We must witness and proclaim this paradoxical kingship as He the King did — that is, by following His own way and striving to adopt His same logic: the logic of humility and service, of the ear of wheat which dies to bear fruit.

[We] are called to be profoundly united first of all in this: All together, under the guidance of the Successor of Peter, [we] must remain in the lordship of Christ, thinking and working in accordance with the logic of the Cross — and this is never easy or predictable.

Homily, Solemnity of Christ the King, November 21, 2010

CHAPTER SEVEN

# Who Was Conceived by the Holy Spirit

## Why Did God Become Man?

Why did God make himself Man? St. Irenaeus writes: "The Word made himself dispenser of the Father's glory for the benefit of men.... The glory of God is the living man — *vivens homo* — and the life of man consists in the vision of God" (*Adv. Haer.* 20: 5, 7).

The glory of God is manifest, therefore, in the salvation of man, whom God so loved as "to give," as the Evangelist John affirms, "His only Son, that whoever believes in Him should not perish but have eternal life" (Jn 3:16). Hence, love is the ultimate reason for the Incarnation of Christ.... The God we contemplate in the crib is God-Love.

General Audience, December 7, 2006

## The Central Mystery of the Faith

The Incarnation of the Son of God is the central mystery of the Christian faith, and in it Mary occupies a central place. But, we ask, what is the meaning of this mystery? And what importance does it have for our concrete lives?

First of all, let us see what the Incarnation means. In the Gospel of St. Luke we heard the words of the angel to Mary: "The Holy Spirit will come upon you, and the power of the Most High will overshadow you; therefore the child to be born will be called holy, the Son of God" (Lk 1:35).

In Mary, the Son of God is made Man, fulfilling in this way the prophecy of Isaiah: "Behold, a young woman shall conceive and bear a son, and shall call his name Immanuel, which means 'God-with-us'" (Is 7:14). Jesus, the Word made flesh, is truly God-with-us, who has come to live among us and to share our human condition.

The Apostle St. John expresses it in the following way: "And the Word became flesh and dwelt among us" (Jn 1:14). The expression "became flesh" points to our human reality in a most concrete and tangible way. In Christ, God has truly come into the world, He has entered into our history, He has set His dwelling among us, thus fulfilling the deepest desire of human beings that the world may truly become a home worthy of humanity.

FOUR-HUNDREDTH ANNIVERSARY MASS
OF THE VIRGIN OF CHARITY OF EL COBRE,
SANTIAGO, CUBA, MARCH 27, 2012

## MARY'S CONSENT TO THE INCARNATION

When God is put aside, the world becomes an inhospitable place for man and frustrates creation's true vocation to be a space for the covenant, for the "yes" to the love between God and humanity who responds to Him. Mary did so as the first fruit of believers with her unreserved "yes" to the Lord.

For this reason, contemplating the mystery of the Incarnation, we cannot fail to turn our eyes to her so as to be filled with wonder, gratitude, and love at seeing how our God, coming into the world, wished to depend upon the free consent of one of His creatures. Only from the moment when the Virgin responded to the angel, "Behold, I am the handmaid of the Lord; let it be to me according to your word" (Lk 1:38), did the eternal Word of the Father begin His human existence in time.

It is touching to see how God not only respects human freedom; He almost seems to require it. And we see also how the beginning of the earthly life of the Son of God was marked by a double "yes" to the saving plan of the Father — that of Christ and that of Mary. This obedience to God is what opens the doors of the world to the truth, to salvation.

God has created us as the fruit of His infinite love. Hence, to live in accordance with His will is the way to encounter our genuine identity, the truth of our being; while apart from God, we are alienated from ourselves and are hurled into the void. The obedience of faith is true liberty, authentic redemption, which allows us to unite ourselves to the love of Jesus in His determination to conform himself to the will of the Father. Redemption is always this process of the lifting up of the human will to full communion with the divine will.

Four-Hundredth Anniversary Mass
of the Virgin of Charity of El Cobre,
Santiago, Cuba, March 27, 2012

## "The Word Became Flesh"

In the Prologue to the Fourth Gospel,... St. John ... meditates profoundly on the mystery of the Incarnation: ... "And the Word became flesh and dwelt among us" (Jn 1:14)....

At Christmas, therefore, we do not limit ourselves to commemorating the birth of a great figure: We do not simply and abstractly celebrate the birth of the man or in general the mystery of life. Even less do we celebrate only the beginning of the new season. At Christmas we commemorate something very tangible and important for mankind, something essential for the Christian faith, a truth that St. John sums up in these few words: "*The Word became flesh*" [Jn 1:14]....

In the darkness of the night of Bethlehem a great light really was lit: The Creator of the universe became flesh, uniting himself indissolubly with human nature so as truly to be "God from God, Light from Light," yet at the same time a Man, true man.

What John calls in Greek *ho logos* [the Word] ... also means "the Meaning." Thus we can understand John's words [this way]: The "eternal Meaning" of the world made himself tangible to our senses and our minds; we may now touch Him and contemplate Him (see 1 Jn 1:1).

The "Meaning" that became flesh is not merely a general idea inherent in the world; it is a "Word" addressed to us. The *Logos* knows us, calls us, guides us. The Word is not a universal law within which we play some role, but rather a Person who is concerned with every individual person: He is the Son of the living God who became man in Bethlehem.

To many people, and in a certain way to all of us, this seems too beautiful to be true. In fact, here it is reaffirmed to us: Yes, a meaning exists, and the meaning is not a powerless protest against the absurd.

The meaning has power: It is God. A good God who must not be confused with any sublime and remote being, whom it would never be possible to reach, but a God who made himself our neighbor and who is very close to us, who has time for each one of us and who came to stay with us.

General Audience, December 17, 2008

CHAPTER EIGHT

# Born of the Virgin Mary

## "Blessed Is She Who Believed"

Dear brothers and sisters, today we praise the Most Holy Virgin for her faith, and with St. Elizabeth we too say, "Blessed is she who believed" (Lk 1:45). As St. Augustine said, Mary conceived Christ by faith in her heart before she conceived Him physically in her womb; Mary believed, and what she believed came to be in her (see *Sermo* 215, 4: PL 38, 1074).

Let us ask the Lord to strengthen our faith, to make it active and fruitful in love. Let us implore Him that, like her, we may welcome the word of God into our hearts, and carry it out with docility and constancy. The Virgin Mary, by her unique role in the mystery of Christ, represents the exemplar and model of the Church. The Church, like the Mother of Christ, is also called to embrace in herself the mystery of God who comes to live in her.

Four-Hundredth Anniversary Mass
of the Virgin of Charity of El Cobre,
Santiago, Cuba, March 27, 2012

## "God With Us"

"A child is born for us, a son is given to us" (Is 9:5). What Isaiah prophesied as he gazed into the future from afar, consoling Israel amid its trials and its darkness, is now proclaimed to the shepherds as a present reality by the angel, from whom a cloud of light streams forth: "To you is born this day in the city of David a Savior, who is Christ the Lord" (Lk 2:11).

The Lord is here. From this moment, God is truly "God with us." No longer is He the distant God who can in some way be perceived from afar, in creation and in our own consciousness. He has entered the world. He is close to us.

The words of the risen Christ to His followers are addressed also to us: "Lo, I am with you always, to the close of the age" (Mt 28:20). For you the Savior is born: Through the Gospel and those who proclaim it, God now reminds us of the message that the angel announced to the shepherds.

It is a message that cannot leave us indifferent. If it is true, it changes everything. If it is true, it also affects me. Like the shepherds, then, I too must say: "Come on, I want to go to Bethlehem to see the Word that has occurred there."

HOMILY, CHRISTMAS MIDNIGHT MASS, DECEMBER 24, 2009

## Making Room for God

"The time came for Mary to be delivered. And she gave birth to her firstborn son and wrapped Him in swaddling clothes, and laid Him in a manger, because there was no room for them in the inn" (Lk 2:6ff). These words touch our hearts every time we hear them.

This was the moment that the angel had foretold at Nazareth: "You will bear a son, and you shall call His name Jesus. He will be great, and will be called the Son of the Most High" (Lk 1:31). This was the moment that Israel had been awaiting for centuries, through many dark hours — the moment that all mankind was somehow awaiting, in terms as yet ill-defined: when God would take care of us, when He would step outside His concealment, when the world would be saved, and God would renew all things.

We can imagine the kind of interior preparation, the kind of love with which Mary approached that hour. The brief phrase "she wrapped him in swaddling clothes" allows us to glimpse something of the holy joy and the silent zeal of that preparation. The swaddling clothes were ready, so that the Child could be given a fitting welcome.

Yet there is no room at the inn. In some way, mankind is awaiting God, waiting for Him to draw near. But when the moment comes, there is no room for him. Man is so preoccupied with himself, he has such urgent need of all the space and all the time for his own things, that nothing remains for others — for his neighbor, for the poor, for God. And the richer men become, the more they fill up all the space by themselves. And the less room there is for others.

St. John, in his Gospel, went to the heart of the matter, giving added depth to St. Luke's brief account of the situation in Bethlehem: "He came to His own home, and His own people received Him not" (Jn 1:11). This refers first and foremost to Bethlehem: The Son of David comes to His own city, but has to be born in a stable, because there is no room for Him at the inn.

Then it refers to Israel: The One who is sent comes among His own, but they do not want Him.

And truly, it refers to all mankind: He through whom the world was made, the primordial Creator-Word, enters into the world, but He is not listened to, He is not received.

These words refer ultimately to us, to each individual and to society as a whole. Do we have time for our neighbor who is in need of a word from us, from me, or in need of my affection? For the sufferer who is in need of help? For the fugitive or the refugee who is seeking asylum?

Do we have time and space for God? Can He enter into our lives? Does He find room in us, or have we occupied all the available space in our thoughts, our actions, our lives for ourselves?

Thank God, this negative detail is not the only one, nor the last one that we find in the Gospel. Just as in Luke we encounter the maternal love of Mary and the fidelity of St. Joseph, the vigilance of the shepherds and their great joy, just as in Matthew we encounter the visit of the wise men, come from afar, so too John says to us: "To all who received Him, He gave power to become children of God" (Jn 1:12). There are those who receive Him, and thus, beginning with the stable, with the outside, there grows silently the new house, the new city, the new world.

Homily, Christmas Midnight Mass, December 24, 2007

## His Light Shines Out

The message of Christmas makes us recognize the darkness of a closed world, and thereby, no doubt, illustrates a reality that we see daily. Yet it also tells us that God does not allow himself to be shut out. He finds a space, even if it means entering through the stable; there are people who see His light and pass it on. Through the word of the Gospel, the angel also speaks to us, and in the sacred liturgy the light of the Redeemer enters our lives.

Whether we are shepherds or "wise men," the light and its message call us to set out, to leave the narrow circle of our desires and interests, to go out to meet the Lord and worship Him. We worship Him by opening the world to truth, to good, to Christ, to the service of those who are marginalized and in whom He awaits us....

In the stable at Bethlehem, Heaven and Earth meet. Heaven has come down to Earth. For this reason, a light shines from the stable for all times; for this reason joy is enkindled there; for this reason song is born there.

With the humility of the shepherds, let us set out … towards the Child in the stable! Then His joy will touch us and will make the world more radiant.

HOMILY, CHRISTMAS MIDNIGHT MASS, DECEMBER 24, 2007

## AWAKEN TO GOD'S PRESENCE

The story of the shepherds is included in the Gospel for a reason. They show us the right way to respond to the message that we too have received. What is it that these first witnesses of God's Incarnation have to tell us?

The first thing we are told about the shepherds is that they were on the watch — they could hear the message precisely because they were awake. We must be awake, so that we can hear the message. We must become truly vigilant people.

What does this mean? The principal difference between someone dreaming and someone awake is that the dreamer is in a world of his own. His "self" is locked into this dream world that is his alone and does not connect him with others. To wake up means to leave that private world of one's own and to enter the common reality, the truth that alone can unite all people.

Conflict and lack of reconciliation in the world stem from the fact that we are locked into our own interests and opinions, into our own little private world. Selfishness, both individual and collective, makes us prisoners of our interests and our desires that stand against the truth and separate us from one another.

Awake, the Gospel tells us. Step outside, so as to enter the great communal truth, the communion of the one God.

To awake, then, means to develop a receptivity for God, for the silent promptings with which He chooses to guide us; for the many indications of His presence.

There are people who describe themselves as "religiously tone deaf." The gift of a capacity to perceive God seems as if it is withheld from some. And indeed — our way of thinking and acting, the mentality of today's world, the whole range of our experience, is inclined to deaden our receptivity for God, to make us "tone deaf" towards Him. And yet in every soul, the desire for God, the capacity to encounter Him, is present, whether in a hidden way or overtly.

In order to arrive at this vigilance, this awakening to what is essential, we should pray for ourselves and for others, for those who appear "tone deaf" and yet in whom there is a keen desire for God to manifest himself.... The Lord himself is present in our midst. Lord, open the eyes of our hearts, so that we may become vigilant and clear-sighted, in this way bringing You close to others as well!

HOMILY, CHRISTMAS MIDNIGHT MASS, DECEMBER 24, 2009

## God Is Most Important

After listening to the angel's message, the shepherds said one to another: "'Let us go over to Bethlehem' ... they went at once" (Lk 2:15–16). "They made haste" is literally what the Greek text says.

What had been announced to them was so important that they had to go immediately. In fact, what had been said to them was utterly out of the ordinary. It changed the world. The Savior is born. The long-awaited Son of David has come into the world in His own city.

What could be more important? No doubt they were partly driven by curiosity. But first and foremost it was their excitement at the wonderful news that had been conveyed to them, of all people, to the little ones, to the seemingly unimportant. They made haste — they went at once.

In our daily life, unfortunately it is not like that. For most people, the things of God are not given priority; they do not impose themselves on us directly. And so the great majority of us tend to postpone them.

First we do what seems urgent here and now. In the list of priorities God is often more or less at the end. We can always deal with that later, we tend to think.

The Gospel tells us: God is the highest priority. If anything in our life deserves haste without delay, then, it is God's work alone....

God is important, by far the most important thing in our lives. The shepherds teach us this priority. From them we should learn not to be crushed by all the pressing matters in our daily lives. From them we should learn the inner freedom to put other tasks in second place — however important they may be — so as to make our way towards God, to allow Him into our lives and into our time.

Time given to God and, in His name, to our neighbor is never time lost. It is the time when we are most truly alive, when we live our humanity to the full.

Homily, Christmas Midnight Mass, December 24, 2009

## Living Close to Christ

Some commentators point out that the shepherds, the simple souls, were the first to come to Jesus in the manger and to encounter the Redeemer of the world. The wise men from the East, representing those with social standing and fame, arrived much later.

These commentators go on to say: This is quite natural. The shepherds lived nearby. They only needed to "come over" (see Lk 2:15), as we do when we go to visit our neighbors.

The wise men, however, lived far away. They had to undertake a long and arduous journey in order to arrive in Bethlehem. And they needed guidance and direction.

Today too there are simple and lowly souls who live very close to the Lord. They are, so to speak, His neighbors, and they can easily go to see Him. But most of us in the world today live far from Jesus Christ, the incarnate God who came to dwell among us. We live our lives by philosophies, amid worldly affairs and occupations that totally absorb us and are a great distance from the Manger.

In all kinds of ways, God has to prod us and reach out to us again and again, so that we can manage to escape from the muddle of our thoughts and activities and discover the way that leads to Him. But a path exists for all of us. The Lord provides everyone with tailor-made signals. He calls each one of us, so that we too can say: "Come on, 'let us go over' to Bethlehem — to the God who has come to meet us."

Yes, indeed, God has set out towards us. Left to ourselves we could not reach Him. The path is too much for our strength.

But God has come down. He comes towards us. He has travelled the longer part of the journey. Now He invites us: Come and see how much I love you. Come and see that I am here....

Let us go there! Let us surpass ourselves! Let us journey towards God in all sorts of ways: along our interior path towards Him, but also along very concrete paths — the Liturgy of the Church, the service of our neighbor, in whom Christ awaits us.

Homily, Christmas Midnight Mass, December 24, 2009

## Is There Something of Herod in Us?

By becoming Man in Mary's womb, the Son of God did not come only for the People of Israel, represented by the shepherds of Bethlehem, but also for the whole of humanity, represented by the Magi.... On the Magi and their journey in search of the Messiah (see Mt 2:1–12) ... the Church invites us to meditate and pray....

We heard in the Gospel that having arrived in Jerusalem from the East, they asked: "Where is He who has been born king of the Jews? For we have seen His star in the East, and have come to worship him" (v. 2)....

King Herod ... was certainly interested in the Child of which the Magi spoke; not in order to worship Him, as he wished to make them believe by lying, but rather to kill Him. Herod was a powerful man who saw others solely as rivals to combat. Basically, on reflection, God also seemed a rival to him, a particularly dangerous rival who would like to deprive men of their vital space, their autonomy, their power; a rival who points out the way to take in life and thus prevents one from doing what one likes.

Herod listened to the interpretations of the prophet Micah's words, made by his experts in Sacred Scripture, but his only thought was of the throne. So God himself had to be clouded over and people had to be reduced to mere pawns to move on the great chessboard of power. Herod is a figure we dislike, whom we instinctively judge negatively because of his brutality.

Yet we should ask ourselves: Is there perhaps something of Herod also in us? Might we too sometimes see God as a sort of rival? Might we too be blind to His signs and deaf to His words because we think He is setting limits on our life and does not allow us to dispose of our existence as we please?

Dear brothers and sisters, when we see God in this way, we end by feeling dissatisfied and discontent because we are not letting ourselves be guided by the One who is the foundation of all things.

We must rid our minds and hearts of the idea of rivalry, of the idea that making room for God is a constraint on us. We must open ourselves to the certainty that God is almighty love that takes nothing away, that does not threaten; on the contrary, He is the only One who can give us the possibility of living to the full, of experiencing true joy.

HOMILY, SOLEMNITY OF THE EPIPHANY, JANUARY 6, 2011

## The Humility of God's Love

Let us follow the journey of the Magi to Jerusalem. Above the great city the star disappears; it is no longer seen. What does this mean? In this case … we must interpret the sign in its depth. For those men it was logical to seek the new king in the royal palace, where the wise court advisors were to be found.

Yet, probably to their amazement, they were obliged to note that this newborn Child was not found in the places of power and culture, even though in those places they were offered precious information about Him.

On the other hand they realized that power, even the power of knowledge, sometimes blocks the way to the encounter with this Child. The star then guided them to Bethlehem, a little town; it led them among the poor and the humble to find the King of the world.

God's criteria differ from human criteria. God does not manifest himself in the power of this world but in the humility of His love, the love that asks our freedom to be welcomed in order to transform us and to enable us to reach the One who is Love.

Homily, Solemnity of the Epiphany, January 6, 2011

## The Son of God and the Mother of God

Christ's nativity … is entirely suffused with the light of Mary and, while we pause at the manger to contemplate the Child, our gaze cannot fail to turn in gratitude also to His Mother, who with her "yes" made possible the gift of redemption. This is why the Christmas Season brings with it a profoundly Marian connotation: The birth of Jesus as God and man and Mary's divine motherhood are inseparable realities. The mystery of Mary and the mystery of the Only-Begotten Son of God who was made man form a single mystery, in which the one helps to better understand the other.

Homily, First Vespers of the Solemnity of Mary,
Mother of God, December 31, 2008

CHAPTER NINE

# Suffered Under Pontius Pilate, Was Crucified, Died, and Was Buried

## The Cross Shows the Father's Love

At the heart of the prayer of blessing [in Eph 1:3ff], the Apostle illustrates the way in which the Father's plan of salvation is brought about in Christ, in His beloved Son. He writes: "In Him we have redemption through His blood, the forgiveness of our trespasses, according to the riches of His grace" (Eph 1:7).

The sacrifice of the cross of Christ is the one and unrepeatable event in which the Father showed His love for us in a luminous way, not only in words but in practice. God is so real and His love is so real that He enters into history, He becomes a Man to feel what it is, how it is to live in this created world; and He accepts the path of suffering of the Passion and even suffers death. God's love is so real that He participates not only in our being but also in our suffering and our dying.

The sacrifice of the Cross ensures that we become "God's property," because the blood of Christ has redeemed us from sin, cleanses us from evil, removes us from the slavery of sin and death. St. Paul invites us to consider the depths of God's love that transforms history, that transformed his very life from being a persecutor of Christians to being an unflagging apostle of the Gospel. Here once again the reassuring words of the Letter to the Romans resound:

"If God is for us, who is against us? He who did not spare His own Son but gave Him up for us all, will He not also give us all things with Him?... For I am sure that neither death, nor life, nor angels, nor principalities, nor things present, nor things to come, nor powers, nor height, nor depth, nor anything else in all creation, will be able to separate us from the love of God in Christ Jesus our Lord" (Rom 8:31–32; 38–39).

We must integrate this certainty — God is for us, and no creature can separate us from Him because His love is stronger — in our being, in our awareness as Christians.

General Audience, June 20, 2012

## "Keep Watch"

Having left the upper room, [Jesus] withdrew to pray, alone before the Father [in the Garden of Gethsemane]. At that moment of deep communion the Gospels recount that Jesus experienced great anguish, such acute suffering that it made Him sweat blood (see Mt 26:38).

In the knowledge of His imminent death on the Cross, He felt immense anguish at the closeness of death. In this situation an element appeared that was of great importance to the whole Church. Jesus said to his followers, "Stay here and keep watch."

This appeal for vigilance concerns precisely this moment of anguish, of threats, in which the traitor was to arrive, but it also concerns the whole history of the Church. It is a permanent message for every era because the disciples' drowsiness was not just a problem at that moment, but is a problem for the whole of history.

The question is this: In what does this apathy consist? What would the watchfulness to which the Lord invites us consist of?

I would say that the disciples' sleepiness in the course of history is a certain insensitiveness of the soul with regard to the power of evil, an insensibility to all the evil in the world. We do not wish to be unduly disturbed by these things; we prefer to forget them. We think that perhaps, after all, it will not be so serious, and we forget.

Moreover, it is not only insensibility to evil, when we should be watchful in order to do good, to fight for the force of goodness. Rather it is an insensibility to God: This is our true sleepiness, this insensibility to God's presence that also makes us insensible to evil. We are not aware of God — He would disturb us — hence we are naturally not aware of the force of evil and continue on the path of our own convenience.

General Audience, April 20, 2011

## "Not My Will, But Yours"

The three Apostles — Peter, James, and John — were asleep [in Gethsemane], but they awoke intermittently and heard the refrain of this prayer of the Lord: "Not *my* will, but *your* will be done." What is this will of *mine,* what is this will of *yours,* of which the Lord speaks?

"My will" is that He should not die, that He be spared this cup of suffering. It is the human will, human nature; and Christ felt, with the whole awareness of His being, His life, the abyss of death, the terror of nothingness, the threat of suffering. Moreover, He was even more acutely aware of the abyss of evil than are we who have a natural aversion to death, a natural fear of death.

Together with death, He felt the whole of humanity's suffering. He felt that this was the cup He was obliged to drink, that He himself had to drink in order to accept the evil of the world, all that is terrible, the aversion to God, the whole weight of sin.

And we can understand that before this reality, the cruelty of which He fully perceived, Jesus, with His human soul, was terrified: My will would be not to drink the cup, but My will is subordinate to Your will, to the will of God, to the will of the Father, which is also the true will of the Son. And thus in this prayer Jesus transformed His natural repugnance, His aversion to the cup and to His mission to die for us. He transformed His own natural will into God's will, into a "yes" to God's will.

Man of himself is tempted to oppose God's will, to seek to do his own will, to feel free only if he is autonomous. He sets his own autonomy against … obeying God's will. This is the whole drama of humanity.

But in truth, this autonomy is mistaken, and entry into God's will is not opposition to the self. It is not a form of slavery that violates my will, but rather means entering into truth and love, into goodness.

And Jesus draws our will — which opposes God's will, which seeks autonomy — upwards, towards God's will. This is the drama of our redemption, that Jesus should uplift our will, our total aversion to God's will and our aversion to death and sin, and unite it with the Father's will: "Not *my* will but *yours*."

In this transformation of "no" into "yes," in this insertion of the creaturely will into the will of the Father, He transforms humanity and redeems us. And He invites us to be part of His movement: to emerge from our "no" and to enter into the "yes" of the Son. My will exists, but the will of the Father is crucial, because it is truth and love.

General Audience, April 20, 2011

## Jesus, the High Priest

The Letter to the Hebrews gave us a profound interpretation of this prayer of the Lord [in] Gethsemane. It says: Jesus' tears, His prayer, His cry, His anguish, all this is not merely a concession to the weakness of the flesh as might be said. It is in this very way that Jesus fulfilled His office as High Priest, because the High Priest must uplift the human being, with all his problems and suffering, to God's heights. And the Letter to the Hebrews says: With all these cries, tears, prayers, and supplications, the Lord has brought our reality to God (see Heb 5:7ff)….

It was in this drama of Gethsemane, where God's power no longer seemed to be present, that Jesus fulfilled His role as High Priest. And it also says that in this act of obedience, that is, of the conforming of the natural human will to God's will, He was perfected as a priest.

Furthermore, it … uses the technical word for ordaining a priest. In this way, He truly became the High Priest of humanity and thus opened heaven and the door to the resurrection.

If we reflect on this drama of Gethsemane we can also see the strong contrast between Jesus — with His anguish, with His suffering — in comparison with the great philosopher Socrates, who stayed calm, without anxiety, in the face of death, which seems the ideal. We can admire this philosopher, but Jesus' mission was different. His mission was not this total indifference and freedom; His mission was to bear in himself the whole burden of our suffering, the whole of the human drama.

This humiliation of Gethsemane, therefore, is essential to the mission of the God-Man. He carries in himself our suffering, our poverty, and transforms it in accordance with God's will. And thus He opens the doors of heaven. He opens heaven: This curtain of the Most Holy One, which until now man has kept closed against God, is opened through His suffering and obedience....

Dear friends, we have endeavored to understand Jesus' state of mind at the moment when He experienced the extreme trial in order to grasp what directed His action. The criterion that throughout His life guided every decision Jesus made was His firm determination to love the Father, to be one with the Father, and to be faithful to Him. This decision to respond to His love impelled Him to embrace the Father's plan in every single circumstance, to make His own the plan of love entrusted to Him, in order to recapitulate all things in God, to lead all things to Him....

Let us also prepare ourselves to welcome God's will in our life, knowing that our own true good, the way to life, is found in God's will, even if it appears harsh in contrast with our intentions. May the Virgin Mother guide us on this itinerary and obtain from her divine Son the grace to be able to spend our life for love of Jesus, in the service of our brethren.

General Audience, April 20, 2011

## "The Foolishness of God"

In ancient culture there did not seem to be room for the message of the Incarnate God. The entire "Jesus of Nazareth" event seemed to be marked by foolishness through and through, and the Cross was certainly its most emblematic point.

But why did St. Paul make precisely this, the word of the Cross, the fundamental core of his teaching? The answer is not difficult: The Cross reveals "the power of God" (1 Cor 1:24), which is different from human power; indeed, it reveals His love: "For the foolishness of God is wiser than men, and the weakness of God is stronger than men" (v. 25).

Centuries after Paul we see that in history it was the Cross that triumphed and not the wisdom that opposed it. The crucified One is wisdom, for He truly shows who God is — that is, a force of love which went even as far as the Cross to save men and women.

God uses ways and means that seem to us at first sight to be merely weakness. The crucified One reveals on the one hand man's frailty, and on the other, the true power of God; that is, the free gift of love: This totally gratuitous love is true wisdom.

St. Paul experienced this even in his flesh and tells us about it in various passages of his spiritual journey, which have become precise reference points for every disciple of Jesus: "He said to me, 'My grace is sufficient for you, for my power is made perfect in weakness'" (2 Cor 12:9); and again, "God chose what is weak in the world to shame the strong" (1 Cor 1:27).

The Apostle identified so closely with Christ that, in spite of being in the midst of so many trials, he too lived in the faith of the Son of God who loved him and gave himself for his sins and for the sins of all (see Gal 1:4; 2:20).

This autobiographical fact concerning the Apostle becomes paradigmatic for all of us.... St. Paul sacrificed his own life, devoting himself without reserve to the ministry of reconciliation, of the Cross, which is salvation for us all. And we too must be able to do this: May we be able to find our strength precisely in the humility of love and our wisdom in the weakness of renunciation, entering thereby into God's power.

We must all model our lives on this true wisdom: We must not live for ourselves but must live in faith in that God of whom we can all say: "He loved me and gave himself for me."

General Audience, October 29, 2008

## Gaze on the Crucified Christ

This evening, in faith, we have accompanied Jesus as He takes the final steps of His earthly journey, the most painful steps, the steps that lead to Calvary. We have heard the cries of the crowd, the words of condemnation, the insults of the soldiers, the lamentation of the Virgin Mary and of the women.

Now we are immersed in the silence of this night, in the silence of the Cross, the silence of death. It is a silence pregnant with the burden of pain borne by a man rejected, oppressed, downtrodden, the burden of sin which mars His face, the burden of evil. Tonight we have relived, deep within our hearts, the drama of Jesus, weighed down by pain, by evil, by human sin.

What remains now before our eyes? It is a crucified Man, a Cross raised on Golgotha, a Cross which seems a sign of the final defeat of the One who brought light to those immersed in darkness, the One who spoke of the power of forgiveness and of mercy, the One who asked us to believe in God's infinite love for each human person. Despised and rejected by men, there stands before us "a man of suffering and acquainted with infirmity, one from whom others hide their faces" (Is 53:3).

But let us look more closely at that man Crucified between earth and heaven. Let us contemplate Him more intently, and we will realize that the Cross is not the banner of death, sin, and evil, but rather the luminous sign of love, of God's immense love, of something that we could never have asked, imagined, or expected: God bent down over us.

Address at the Coliseum after the Way of the Cross,
April 22, 2011

## Seed of New Hope

[God] lowered himself, even to the darkest corner of our lives, in order to stretch out His hand and draw us to himself, to bring us all the way to himself. The Cross speaks to us of the supreme love of God and invites us, today, to renew our faith in the power of that love, and to believe that in every situation of our lives, our history, and our world, God is able to vanquish death, sin, and evil, and to give us new, risen life. In the Son of God's death on the Cross, we find the seed of new hope for life, like the seed which dies within the earth.

This night full of silence, full of hope, echoes God's call to us as found in the words of St. Augustine: "Have faith! You will come to me and you will taste the good things of My table, even as I did not disdain to taste the evil things of your table.… I have promised you my own life.

"As a pledge of this, I have given you my death, as if to say: Look! I am inviting you to share in my life. It is a life where no one dies, a life which is truly blessed, which offers an incorruptible food, the food which refreshes and never fails. The goal to which I invite you … is friendship with the

Father and the Holy Spirit, it is the eternal supper, it is communion with me.... It is a share in my own life" (see *Sermo* 231, 5).

Let us gaze on the crucified Jesus, and let us ask in prayer: Enlighten our hearts, Lord, that we may follow you along the Way of the Cross. Put to death in us the "old man" bound by selfishness, evil, and sin. Make us "new men," men and women of holiness, transformed and enlivened by your love.

ADDRESS AT THE COLISEUM AFTER THE WAY OF THE CROSS,
APRIL 22, 2011

## He Has Entered into Our Grief

The anguish of the passion of the Lord Jesus cannot fail to move to pity even the most hardened hearts, as it constitutes the climax of the revelation of God's love for each of us. St. John observes: "God so loved the world that He gave His only Son, that whoever believes in Him should not perish, but have eternal life" (Jn 3:16). It is for love of us that Christ dies on the cross!

Throughout the course of the millennia, a great multitude of men and women have been drawn deeply into this mystery, and they have followed Him, making in their turn, like Him and with His help, a gift to others of their own lives. They are the saints and the martyrs, many of whom remain unknown to us. Even in our own time, how many people, in the silence of their daily lives, unite their sufferings with those of the crucified One and become apostles of a true spiritual and social renewal!

What would man be without Christ? St. Augustine observes: "You would still be in a state of wretchedness, had He not shown you mercy. You would not have returned to life, had He not shared your death. You would have passed away had He not come to your aid. You would be lost, had He not come" (*Discourse* 185:1). So why not welcome Him into our lives?

Let us pause this evening to contemplate His disfigured face: It is the face of the Man of Sorrows, who took upon himself the burden of all our mortal anguish. His face is reflected in that of every person who is humiliated and offended, sick and suffering, alone, abandoned, and despised. Pouring out His blood, He has rescued us from the slavery of death; He has broken the solitude of our tears; He has entered into our every grief and our every anxiety.

Address at the Coliseum after the Way of the Cross,
April 22, 2011

## "Why Have You Forsaken Me?"

What is the meaning of Jesus' prayer, of the cry He addresses to the Father: "My God, my God, why have you forsaken me?" (Mk 15:33–34). Doubt about His mission, about the Father's presence? Might there not be in this prayer the knowledge that He had been forsaken?

The words that Jesus addresses to the Father are the beginning of Psalm 22, in which the Psalmist expresses to God his being torn between feeling forsaken and the certain knowledge of God's presence in His people's midst. He, the Psalmist, prays: "O my God, I cry by day, but you do not answer; and by night, but find no rest. Yet you are holy, enthroned on the praises of Israel" (vv. 3–4). The Psalmist speaks of this "cry" in order to express the full suffering of his prayer to God, seemingly absent: In the moment of anguish his prayer becomes a cry.

This also happens in our relationship with the Lord: When we face the most difficult and painful situations, when it seems that God does not hear, we must not be afraid to entrust the whole weight of our overburdened hearts to Him, we must not fear to cry out to Him in our suffering, we must be convinced that God is close, even if He seems silent.

Repeating from the Cross the first words of Psalm 22, "*Eli, Eli, lama sabachthani?*" — "My God my God, why have you forsaken me?" (Mt 27:46) — uttering the words of the Psalm, Jesus prays at the moment of His ultimate rejection by men, at the moment of abandonment. Yet He prays, with the Psalm, in the awareness of God's presence, even in that hour when He is feeling the human drama of death.

General Audience, February 8, 2012

## Suffering with Us and for Us

A question arises within us: How is it possible that such a powerful God does not intervene to save His Son from this terrible trial [on the Cross]?

It is important to understand that Jesus' prayer ["My God my God, why have you forsaken me?" (Mt 27:46)] is not the cry of one who meets death with despair, nor is it the cry of one who knows He has been forsaken. At this moment Jesus makes His own the whole of Psalm 22, the psalm of the suffering people of Israel. In this way He takes upon himself not only the sin of His people, but also that of all men and women who are suffering from the oppression of evil; and at the same time, He places all this before God's own heart, in the certainty that His cry will be heard in the Resurrection....

In this prayer of Jesus are contained His extreme trust and His abandonment into God's hands, even when God seems absent, even when He seems to be silent, complying with a plan incomprehensible to us.... His is a suffering in communion with us and for us, which derives from love and already bears within it redemption, the victory of love....

At the supreme moment, Jesus gives vent to His heart's grief, but at the same time makes clear the meaning of the Father's presence and His consent to the Father's plan of the salvation of humanity.

We too have to face ever anew the "today" of suffering of God's silence — we express it so often in our prayers — but we also find ourselves facing the "today" of the Resurrection, of the response of God who took upon himself our sufferings, to carry them together with us and to give us the firm hope that they will be overcome (see Encyclical Letter *Spe Salvi*, nn. 35–40).

Dear friends, let us lay our daily crosses before God in our prayers, in the certainty that He is present and hears us. Jesus' cry reminds us that in prayer we must surmount the barriers of our "ego" and our problems, and open ourselves to the needs and suffering of others.

May the prayer of Jesus dying on the Cross teach us to pray lovingly for our many brothers and sisters who are oppressed by the weight of daily life, who are living through difficult moments, who are in pain, who have no word of comfort. Let us place all this before God's heart, so that they too may feel the love of God who never abandons us.

General Audience, February 8, 2012

## "Into Your Hands I Commit My Spirit"

At this moment of suffering [on the Cross], Jesus' prayer, "Father, into your hands I commit my spirit," is a loud cry of supreme and total entrustment to God. This prayer expresses the full awareness that He had not been abandoned.

The initial invocation — "Father" — recalls His first declaration as a twelve-year-old boy. At that time He had stayed for three days in the temple of Jerusalem, whose veil was now torn in two. And when His parents had told Him of their anxiety, He had answered: "How is it that you sought me? Did you not know that I must be in my Father's house?" (Lk 2:49).

From the beginning to the end, what fully determines Jesus' feelings, words, and actions is His unique relationship with the Father. On the Cross He lives to the full, in love, this filial relationship He has with God, which gives life to His prayer.

The words spoken by Jesus after his invocation "Father" borrow a sentence from Psalm 31: "Into your hands I commit my spirit" (Ps 31:6). Yet these words are not a mere citation, but rather express a firm decision: Jesus "delivers" himself to the Father in an act of total abandonment.

These words are a prayer of "entrustment," total trust in God's love. Jesus' prayer as He faces death is dramatic, as it is for every human being. But at the same time, it is imbued with that deep calmness that is born from trust in the Father and from the desire to commend oneself totally to Him.

In Gethsemane, when He had begun His final struggle and His most intense prayer, and was about to be "delivered into the hands of men" (Lk 9:44), His sweat had become "like great drops of blood falling down upon the ground" (Lk 22:44). Nevertheless, His heart was fully obedient to the Father's will, and because of this "an angel from heaven" came to strengthen Him (see Lk 22:42–43). Now, in His last moments, Jesus turns to the Father, telling Him into whose hands He really commits His whole life.

Before starting out on His journey towards Jerusalem, Jesus had insisted to His disciples: "Let these words sink into your ears; for the Son of Man is to be delivered into the hands of men" (Lk 9:44).

Now that life is about to depart from Him, He seals His last decision in prayer: Jesus let himself be delivered "into the hands of men," but it is into the hands of the Father that He places His spirit. Thus — as the Evangelist John affirms — all was finished, the supreme act of love was carried to the end, to the limit and beyond the limit.

Dear brothers and sisters, the words of Jesus on the Cross at the last moments of His earthly life offer us demanding instructions for our prayers, but they also open us to serene trust and firm hope. Jesus, who asks the Father to forgive those who are crucifying Him, invites us to take the difficult step of also praying for those who wrong us, who have injured us, ever able to forgive, so that God's light may illuminate their hearts. And He invites us to live in our prayers the same attitude of mercy and love with which God treats us: "Forgive us our trespasses and forgive those who trespass against us," we say every day in the Lord's Prayer.

At the same time, Jesus, who at the supreme moment of death entrusts himself totally to the hands of God the Father, communicates to us the certainty that, however harsh the trial, however difficult the problems, however acute the suffering may be, we shall never fall from God's hands, those hands that created us, that sustain us, and that accompany us on our way through life, because they are guided by an infinite and faithful love.

General Audience, February 15, 2012

CHAPTER TEN

# He Descended into Hell

## The Key to the Gates of Death

In the Creed, we say about Christ's journey that He "descended into hell." What happened then?

Since we have no knowledge of the world of death, we can only imagine His triumph over death with the help of images that remain very inadequate. Yet, inadequate as they are, they can help us to understand something of the mystery.

The liturgy applies to Jesus' descent into the night of death the words of Psalm 24: "Lift up your heads, O gates; be lifted up, O ancient doors!" The gates of death are closed; no one can return from there. There is no key for those iron doors.

But Christ has the key [see Rev 1:17–18]. His cross opens wide the gates of death, the stern doors. They are barred no longer. His cross, His radical love, is the key that opens them. The love of the One who, though God, became Man in order to die — this love has the power to open those doors. This love is stronger than death.

The Easter icons of the Oriental Church show how Christ enters the world of the dead. He is clothed with light, for God is light. "The night is bright as the day, the darkness is as light" (Ps 139:12).

Entering the world of the dead, Jesus bears the stigmata, the signs of His passion. His wounds, His suffering, have become power; they are love that conquers death. He meets Adam and all the men and women waiting in the night of death. As we look at them, we can hear an echo of the prayer of Jonah: "Out of the belly of Sheol I cried, and you heard my voice" (Jonah 2:2).

In the Incarnation, the Son of God became one with human beings — with Adam. But only at this moment, when He accomplishes the supreme act of love by descending into the night of death, does He bring the journey of the Incarnation to its completion. By His death He now clasps the hand of Adam, of every man and woman who awaits Him, and brings them to the light.

But we may ask: What is the meaning of all this imagery? What was truly new in what happened on account of Christ? The human soul was created immortal — what exactly did Christ bring that was new?

The soul is indeed immortal, because man in a unique way remains in God's memory and love, even after his fall. But his own powers are insufficient to lift him up to God. We lack the wings needed to carry us to those heights.

And yet, nothing else can satisfy man eternally, except being with God. An eternity without this union with God would be a punishment. Man cannot attain those heights on his own, yet he yearns for them. "Out of the depths I cry to you." …

Only the risen Christ can bring us to complete union with God, to the place where our own powers are unable to bring us. Truly, Christ puts the lost sheep upon His shoulders and carries it home. Clinging to His Body we have life, and in communion with His Body we reach the very heart of God. Only thus is death conquered, we are set free, and our life is hope.

Homily, Easter Vigil, April 7, 2007

## Love Is Stronger Than Death

This is the joy of the Easter Vigil: We are free. In the resurrection of Jesus, love has been shown to be stronger than death, stronger than evil. Love made Christ descend, and love is also the power by which He ascends, the power by which He brings us with Him.

In union with His love, borne aloft on the wings of love, as persons of love, let us descend with Him into the world's darkness, knowing that in this way we will also rise up with Him....

Let us pray: Lord, show us that love is stronger than hatred, that love is stronger than death. Descend into the darkness and the abyss of our modern age, and take by the hand those who await You. Bring them to the light!

In my own dark nights, be with me to bring me forth! Help me, help all of us, to descend with You into the darkness of all those people who are still waiting for You, who out of the depths cry unto You! Help us to bring them your light! Help us to say the "yes" of love, the love that makes us descend with you and, in so doing, also to rise with You. Amen!

Homily, Easter Vigil, April 7, 2007

## "I Am with You"

From ancient times the liturgy of Easter day has begun with the [Latin] words: *Resurrexi et adhuc tecum sum* ("I arose, and am still with you; you have set your hand upon me.") The liturgy sees these as the first words spoken by the Son to the Father after His resurrection, after His return from the night of death into the world of the living. The hand of the Father upheld Him even on that night, and thus He could rise again.

These words are taken from Psalm 138, where originally they had a different meaning. That psalm is a song of wonder at God's omnipotence and omnipresence, a hymn of trust in the God who never allows us to fall from His hands. And His hands are good hands.

The Psalmist imagines himself journeying to the farthest reaches of the cosmos — and what happens to him? "If I ascend to heaven, you are there! If I make my bed in Sheol [the realm of the dead], you are there! If I take the wings of the morning and dwell in the uttermost parts of the sea, even there your hand shall lead me, and your right hand shall hold me. If I say, 'Let only darkness cover me'…, even the darkness is not dark to you…; for darkness is as light with you" (Ps 139:8–12).

On Easter day the Church tells us that Jesus Christ made that journey to the ends of the universe for our sake. In the Letter to the Ephesians we read that He descended to the depths of the earth, and that the one who descended is also the One who has risen far above the heavens, that He might fill all things (see Eph 4:9ff).

The vision of the psalm thus became reality. In the impenetrable gloom of death Christ came like light — the night became as bright as day and the darkness became as light.

And so the Church can rightly consider these words of thanksgiving and trust as words spoken by the risen Lord to his Father: "Yes, I have journeyed to the uttermost depths of the earth, to the abyss of death, and brought them light; now I have risen and I am upheld forever by your hands."

But these words of the risen Christ to the Father have also become words that the Lord speaks to us: "I arose and now I am still with you," He says to each of us. "My hand upholds you. Wherever you may fall, you will always fall into my hands. I am present even at the door of death. Where no one can accompany you further, and where you can bring nothing, even there I am waiting for you, and for you I will change darkness into light."

HOMILY, EASTER VIGIL, APRIL 7, 2007

## HOLY SATURDAY, WHEN GOD REMAINS HIDDEN

One could say that the Shroud [of Turin] is the ... Icon of Holy Saturday. Indeed it is a winding-sheet that was wrapped round the body of a man who was crucified, corresponding in every way to what the Gospels tell us of Jesus who, crucified at about noon, died at about three o'clock in the afternoon. At nightfall, since it was ... the eve of Holy Saturday, Joseph of Arimathea, a rich and authoritative member of the Sanhedrin, courageously asked Pontius Pilate for permission to bury Jesus in his new tomb, which he had hewn out in the rock not far from Golgotha.

Having obtained permission, he bought a linen cloth, and after Jesus was taken down from the Cross, wrapped Him in that shroud and buried Him in that tomb (see Mk 15:42–46). This is what the Gospel of St. Mark says, and the other Evangelists are in agreement with him.

From that moment, Jesus remained in the tomb until dawn of the day after the Sabbath, and the Turin Shroud presents to us an image of how His body lay in the tomb during that period — which was chronologically brief (about a day and a half), but immense, infinite in its value and in its significance.

Holy Saturday is the day when God remains hidden, as we read in an ancient homily: "What has happened? Today the earth is shrouded in deep silence, deep silence and stillness, profound silence because the King sleeps.... God has died in the flesh, and has gone down to rouse the realm of the dead." ... In the Creed, we profess that Jesus Christ was "crucified under Pontius Pilate, died and was buried. He descended to the dead. On the third day, He rose again."

Dear brothers and sisters, in our time, especially after having lived through the past century, humanity has become particularly sensitive to the mystery of Holy Saturday. The concealment of God is part of contemporary man's spirituality, in an existential, almost subconscious manner, like a void in the heart that has continued to grow larger and larger.

Towards the end of the 19th century, [the German philosopher Friedrich] Nietzsche wrote: "God is dead! And we killed him!" This famous saying is clearly taken almost literally from the Christian tradition. We often repeat it in the Way of the Cross, perhaps without being fully aware of what we are saying.

After the two World Wars, the *lagers* and the *gulags*, Hiroshima and Nagasaki, our epoch has become — increasingly — a Holy Saturday: This day's darkness challenges all who are wondering about life, and it challenges us believers in particular. We too have something to do with this darkness.

Yet the death of the Son of God, Jesus of Nazareth, has an opposite aspect, totally positive, a source of comfort and hope. And this reminds me of the fact that the Holy Shroud acts as a "photographic" document, with both a "positive" and a "negative." And in fact, this is really how it is: The darkest mystery of faith is at the same time the most luminous sign of a never-ending hope.

MEDITATION ON THE SHROUD OF TURIN, MAY 2, 2010

## "The Passion of Christ, the Passion of Man"

Holy Saturday is a "no man's land" between death and resurrection, but this "no man's land" was entered by One, the only One, who passed through it with the signs of His passion for man's sake. *Passio Christi. Passio hominis.* ["The passion of Christ, the passion of man."] And the Shroud [of Turin] speaks to us precisely about this moment — testifying exactly to that unique and unrepeatable interval in the history of humanity and the universe in which God, in Jesus Christ, not only shared our dying but also our remaining in death — the most radical solidarity.

In this "time beyond time," Jesus Christ "descended to the dead." What do these words mean? They mean that God, having made himself man, reached the point of entering man's most extreme and absolute solitude, where not a ray of love enters, where total abandonment reigns without any word of comfort: "hell." Jesus Christ, by remaining in death, passed beyond the door of this ultimate solitude to lead us too to cross it with Him.

We have all, at some point, felt the frightening sensation of abandonment, and that is what we fear most about death, just as when we were children we were afraid to be alone in the dark and could only be reassured by the presence of a person who loved us.

Well, this is exactly what happened on Holy Saturday: The voice of God resounded in the realm of death. The unimaginable occurred: Namely, Love penetrated "hell."

Even in the extreme darkness of the most absolute human loneliness, we may hear a voice that calls us and find a hand that takes ours and leads us out. Human beings live because they are loved and can love; and if love penetratec even the realm of death, then life also even reached there. In the hour of supreme solitude we shall never be alone: *Passio Christi. Passio hominis.*

This is the mystery of Holy Saturday! Truly from there, from the darkness of the death of the Son of God, the light of a new hope gleamed: the light of the Resurrection. And it seems to me that, looking at this sacred cloth through the eyes of faith, one may perceive something of this light.

Effectively, the Shroud was immersed in that profound darkness that was at the same time luminous; and I think that if thousands and thousands of people come to venerate it — without counting those who contemplate it through images — it is because they see in it not only darkness but also the light; not so much the defeat of life and of love, but rather victory, the *victory* of life over death, of love over hatred. They indeed see the death of Jesus, but they also see His resurrection; in the bosom of death, life is now vibrant, since Love dwells within it.

This is the power of the Shroud: From the face of this "Man of Sorrows," who carries with Him the passion of man of every time and every place, our passions too, our sufferings, our difficulties and our sins — *Passio Christi. Passio hominis* — from this face a solemn majesty shines, a paradoxical lordship. This face, these hands and these feet, this side, this whole body speaks. It is itself a word we can hear in the silence.

How does the Shroud speak? It speaks with blood, and blood is life! The Shroud is an icon written in blood: the blood of a man who was scourged, crowned with thorns, crucified, and whose right side was pierced. The image impressed upon the Shroud is that of a dead man, but the blood speaks of His life.

of blood speaks of love and of life — espe-
stain near His rib, made by the blood and
owed copiously from a great wound inflicted by
a Roman spear. That blood and that water speak
o. it is like a spring that murmurs in the silence, and we
can hear it, we can listen to it in the silence of Holy Saturday.

MEDITATION ON THE SHROUD OF TURIN, MAY 2, 2010

## THE MEDICINE OF IMMORTALITY

An ancient Jewish legend from the apocryphal book *The Life of Adam and Eve* recounts that, in his final illness, Adam sent his son Seth together with Eve into the region of Paradise to fetch the oil of mercy, so that he could be anointed with it and healed. The two of them went in search of the tree of life, and after much praying and weeping on their part, the Archangel Michael appeared to them, and told them they would not obtain the oil of the tree of mercy and that Adam would have to die.

Later, Christian readers added a word of consolation to the Archangel's message, to the effect that after 5,500 years the loving King, Christ, would come, the Son of God who would anoint all those who believe in Him with the oil of His mercy: "The oil of mercy from eternity to eternity will be given to those who are reborn of water and the Holy Spirit. Then the Son of God, Christ, abounding in love, will descend into the depths of the earth and will lead your father into Paradise, to the tree of mercy."

This legend lays bare the whole of humanity's anguish at the destiny of illness, pain, and death that has been imposed upon us. Man's resistance to death becomes evident: Somewhere — people have constantly thought — there must be some cure for death. Sooner or later it should be possible to find the remedy not only for this or that illness, but for our ultimate destiny — for death itself. Surely the medicine of immortality must exist.

Today, too, the search for a source of healing continues. Modern medical science strives, if not exactly to exclude death, at least to eliminate as many as possible of its causes, to postpone it further and further, to prolong life more and more.

But let us reflect for a moment: What would it really be like if we were to succeed, perhaps not in excluding death totally, but in postponing it indefinitely, in reaching an age of several hundred years? Would that be a good thing?

Humanity would become extraordinarily old. There would be no more room for youth. Capacity for innovation would die, and endless life would be no paradise — if anything, it would be a condemnation.

The true cure for death must be different. It cannot lead simply to an indefinite prolongation of this current life. It would have to transform our lives from within. It would need to create a new life within us, truly fit for eternity: It would need to transform us in such a way as not to come to an end with death, but only then to begin in fullness.

What is new and exciting in the Christian message, in the Gospel of Jesus Christ, was and is that we are told: Yes, indeed, this cure for death, this true medicine of immortality, does exist. It has been found. It is within our reach.... Christ is the tree of life, once more within our reach. If we remain close to him, then we have life.

Homily, Easter Vigil, April 3, 2010

CHAPTER ELEVEN

# On the Third Day He Rose Again from the Dead

## The "Good News" Par Excellence

After the weeping and distress of Good Friday and after the silence, laden with expectation, of Holy Saturday, here is the wonderful announcement: "The Lord has risen indeed, and has appeared to Simon!" (Lk 24:34).

This is the "Good News" par excellence in the entire history of the world. It is the "Gospel" proclaimed and passed on down the centuries, from generation to generation.

Christ's Pasch [Passover] is the supreme and unequalled act of God's power. It is an absolutely extraordinary event, the most beautiful, ripe fruit of the "Mystery of God." It is so extraordinary that it is ineffable in its dimensions that escape our human capacity for knowing and investigating.

Yet it is also an "historical" event, witnessed to and documented. It is the event on which the whole of our faith is founded. It is the central content in which we believe and the main reason why we believe.

The New Testament does not describe how the resurrection of Jesus took place. It only mentions the testimonies of those whom Jesus met personally after He had risen. The three Synoptic Gospels tell us that this announcement — "He has risen!" — was first proclaimed by angels. It is therefore a proclamation that originates in God; but God immediately entrusts it to His "messengers," so that they may pass it on to all.

Hence it is these same angels who tell the women, who had gone at daybreak to the tomb, "Go quickly and tell His disciples that He has risen from the dead, and behold, He is going before you to Galilee; there you will see Him" (Mt 28:7). In this way, through the women of the Gospel, this divine mandate reaches each and every one so that each in turn may transmit this same news to others with faithfulness and courage: the glad tidings that are joyful and convey delight.

Yes, dear friends, our whole faith is founded on the constant and faithful transmission of this "Good News," and today we want to tell God of our deep gratitude for the innumerable hosts of believers in Christ who have gone before us in the course of the centuries, because they never failed in their fundamental mandate to proclaim the Gospel which they had received.

General Audience, April 7, 2010

## Courageous Witnesses

The Good News of Easter ... requires the action of enthusiastic and courageous witnesses. Each disciple of Christ, and also each one of us, is called to be a witness. This is the precise, demanding, and exalting mandate of the Risen Lord.

The "news" of new life in Christ must shine out in the life of Christians, it must be alive and active in those who bring it, really capable of changing hearts and the whole of life.

It is alive first of all because Christ himself is its living and life-giving soul. St. Mark reminds us, at the end of his Gospel, where he writes that the Apostles "went forth and preached everywhere, while the Lord worked with them and confirmed the message by the signs that attended it" (Mk 16:20).

The Apostles' experience is also our own and that of every believer, of every disciple who makes himself a "herald." In fact, we too are sure that the Lord works with His witnesses today, as He did in the past. This is a fact we can recognize every time we see the seeds of true and lasting peace sprouting, and wherever the work and example of Christians and of people of good will is enlivened by respect for justice, patient dialogue, convinced esteem for others, impartiality, and personal and communitarian renunciation.

Unfortunately, we also see in the world so much suffering, so much violence, so much misunderstanding. The celebration of the Paschal Mystery, the joyous contemplation of Christ's resurrection that triumphs over sin and death with the power of God's love, is a favorable opportunity for rediscovering and professing with greater conviction and trust in the risen Lord, who accompanies the witnesses of His word, working miracles together with them.

We shall be truly and with our whole selves witnesses of the risen Jesus when we let the wonder of His love shine through us: When in our words, and especially in our actions, the voice and hand of Jesus Himself may be recognized as fully consistent with the Gospel.

General Audience, April 7, 2010

## Light Is Created Anew

Easter is the feast of the new creation. Jesus is risen and dies no more. He has opened the door to a new life, one that no longer knows illness and death. He has taken mankind up into God himself.... A new dimension has opened up for mankind. Creation has become greater and broader....

What the Church hears on Easter night is above all the first element of the creation account: "God said, 'Let there be light!'" (Gen 1:3). The creation account begins symbolically with the creation of light....

What is the creation account saying here? Light makes life possible. It makes encounter possible. It makes communication possible. It makes knowledge, access to reality and to truth, possible. And insofar as it makes knowledge possible, it makes freedom and progress possible.

Evil hides. Light, then, is also an expression of the good that both is and creates brightness. It is daylight, which makes it possible for us to act.

To say that God created light means that God created the world as a space for knowledge and truth, as a space for encounter and freedom, as a space for good and for love. Matter is fundamentally good, being itself is good. And evil does not come from God-made being; rather, it comes into existence only through denial. It is a "no."

At Easter, on the morning of the first day of the week, God said once again: "Let there be light." The night on the Mount of Olives, the solar eclipse of Jesus' passion and death, the night of the grave had all passed. Now it is the first day once again — creation is beginning anew.

"Let there be light," says God, "and there was light": Jesus rises from the grave. Life is stronger than death. Good is stronger than evil. Love is stronger than hate. Truth is stronger than lies.

The darkness of the previous days is driven away the moment Jesus rises from the grave and himself becomes God's pure light. But this applies not only to Him, not only to the darkness of those days. With the resurrection of Jesus, light itself is created anew. He draws all of us after Him into the new light of the Resurrection, and He conquers all darkness. He is God's new day, new for all of us.

Homily, Easter Vigil, April 7, 2012

## The Paschal Candle

On Easter night, the night of the new creation, the Church presents the mystery of light using a unique and very humble symbol: the Paschal candle. This is a light that lives from sacrifice. The candle shines inasmuch as it is burnt up. It gives light, inasmuch as it gives itself. Thus the Church presents most beautifully the paschal mystery of Christ, who gives himself and so bestows the great light....

We should remember that the light of the candle is a fire. Fire is the power that shapes the world, the force of transformation. And fire gives warmth. Here too the mystery of Christ is made newly visible. Christ, the light, is fire, flame, burning up evil and so reshaping both the world and ourselves.... And this fire is both heat and light: not a cold light, but one through which God's warmth and goodness reach down to us.

Let us pray to the Lord at this time that He may grant us to experience the joy of His light; let us pray that we ourselves may become bearers of His light, and that through the Church, Christ's radiant face may enter our world.

Homily, Easter Vigil, April 7, 2012

## He Will Call Us by Name

In these days [after Easter], the liturgy recalls Jesus' various encounters after His resurrection: with Mary Magdalene and the other women who went to the tomb at the crack of dawn the day after the Sabbath; with the Apostles who gathered, unbelieving, in the Upper Room; with Thomas and other disciples.

Christ's different apparitions are also an invitation to us today to deepen the fundamental message of Easter: They are an incentive to us to retrace the spiritual journey of those who encountered Christ and recognized Him in those first days following the Paschal events.

The Evangelist John recounts that when Peter and he heard Mary Magdalene's news, they ran to the sepulcher, each trying as it were to outstrip the other (see Jn 20:3ff). The Fathers of the Church have seen in their haste to reach the empty tomb an exhortation to compete in the only legitimate race between believers: the competition in seeking Christ.

And what can be said of Mary Magdalene? She stood weeping by the empty tomb with the sole desire to know where they had taken her Lord. She encounters Him and recognizes Him only when He calls her by name (see Jn 20:11–18). If we seek the Lord with a simple and sincere mind, we too will find Him; indeed, He himself will come to meet us. He will make us recognize Him, He will call us by name; that is, He will admit us to the intimacy of his love.

HOMILY, OCTAVE OF EASTER, APRIL 11, 2007

## THE DISCIPLES AT EMMAUS

On Wednesday in the Octave of Easter, the liturgy has us meditate on another unique encounter with the risen One, that of the two disciples at Emmaus (see Lk 24:13–35).

While they were going home, distressed by the death of their Master, the Lord kept them company on the way without their recognizing Him. His words, as He commented on the Scriptures that concerned Him, made the hearts of the two disciples burn within them, and on reaching their destination they asked Him to stay with them. When finally He "took the bread and blessed and broke it, and gave it to them" (v. 30), their eyes were opened.

Yet, at that very instant Jesus vanished from their sight. Thus they recognized Him when He disappeared.

Commenting on this Gospel episode, St. Augustine observes: "Jesus broke the bread, they recognized Him. Then we should no longer say that we do not know Christ! If we believe, we know Him! Indeed, if we believe, we have Him! They had Christ at their table; we have Him in our souls!"

And he concludes: "Having Christ in one's own heart is far more than having him in one's house: In fact, our hearts are more intimate to us than our homes" (*Sermon* 232, VII, 7). Let us truly seek to carry Jesus in our heart.

HOMILY, OCTAVE OF EASTER, APRIL 11, 2007

## CHRIST HAS "PASSED OVER"

In the prologue to the Acts of the Apostles, St. Luke said that the risen Lord "presented himself [to the Apostles] alive after His passion by many proofs, appearing to them during forty days" (Acts 1:3). It is necessary to understand properly that when the sacred author says "He presented himself alive," he does not mean that Jesus returned to the same life that He had lived before, as Lazarus had done.

The Pasch [Passover] that we celebrate, St. Bernard remarks, means "passing" and not "returning," for Jesus did not return to His previous situation, but "crossed a boundary to a more glorious condition," new and definitive. For this reason he adds: "Christ has now truly passed over to a new life" (see *Homily on Easter*).

To Mary Magdalene the Lord said: "Do not hold me, for I have not yet ascended to the Father" (Jn 20:17). These words surprise us, especially if we compare them to what, on the other hand, happened to doubting Thomas. There in the Upper Room, the risen One himself presented His hands and His side to the Apostle so that he could touch them and thereby be sure that it was truly He (see Jn 20:27).

In fact, the two episodes are not contradictory. On the contrary, the one helps us to understand the other.

Mary Magdalene would have wanted to have her Lord as He was before, considering the Cross a tragic memory to be forgotten. Henceforth, however, there was no longer room for a merely human relationship with the risen One.

To meet Him, we must not turn back, but relate to Him in a new way. We must move ahead! St. Bernard underlines this: Jesus "invites us all to this new life, to this passing.... We will not see Christ with a backward glance" (*Homily on Easter*).

This is what happened with Thomas. Jesus showed him His wounds, not to make him forget the Cross, but to make it unforgettable in the future, too.

It is towards the future, in fact, that we now turn our gaze. The disciple's task is to witness to the death and resurrection of his Master and to His new life. For this reason Jesus invited His unbelieving friend to "touch" Him: He wanted him to witness directly to His resurrection.

Dear brothers and sisters, we too, like Mary Magdalene, Thomas, and the other apostles, are called to be witnesses of Christ's death and resurrection. We cannot keep this important news to ourselves. We must convey it to the whole world: "We have seen the Lord!" (Jn 20:25).

Homily, Octave of Easter, April 11, 2007

CHAPTER TWELVE

# He Ascended into Heaven

## He Is Close to Us Forever

So what does the Feast of the Ascension of the Lord mean for us? It does not mean that the Lord has departed to some place far from people and from the world. Christ's ascension is not a journey into space toward the most remote stars; for basically, the planets, like the earth, are also made of physical elements.

Christ's ascension means that He no longer belongs to the world of corruption and death that conditions our life. It means that He belongs entirely to God. He, the eternal Son, led our human existence into God's presence, taking with Him flesh and blood in a transfigured form.

The human being finds room in God; through Christ, the human being was introduced into the very life of God. And since God embraces and sustains the entire cosmos, the ascension of the Lord means that Christ has not departed from us, but that He is now, thanks to His being with the Father, close to each one of us forever.

Each one of us can be on intimate terms with Him; each can call upon Him. The Lord is always within hearing. We can inwardly draw away from Him. We can live turning our backs on him. But He always waits for us and is always close to us.

Homily, Mass of Possession of the Chair, May 7, 2005

## Humanity Is Raised to God

According to the Book of the Acts of the Apostles, forty days after the Resurrection, Jesus ascended into heaven: That is, He returned to the Father, by whom He had been sent into the world.... The Ascension of the Lord marks the completion of the salvation that began with the Incarnation.

After having instructed His disciples for the last time, Jesus ascended into heaven (see Mark 16:19). However, He "did not separate himself from our condition";... in fact, in His humanity, He brought humanity with Him into the depths of the Father, and thus revealed the final destination of our earthly pilgrimage. Just as He descended from heaven for us, and suffered and died for us on the cross, so too He rose from the dead and ascended to God for us. And so God is no longer distant but is "our God," "our Father" (see Jn 20:17).

The ascension is the ultimate act of our liberation from sin; as St. Paul writes: "He ascended on high and took prisoners captive" (Eph 4:8). St. Leo the Great explains that with this mystery "not only is there proclaimed the immortality of the soul, but also that of the flesh. Today, in fact, we are not only confirmed as possessors of paradise, but we have with Christ penetrated the heights of heaven" (*De Ascensione Domini, Tractatus* 73, 2.4: CCL 138 A, 451.453).

This is why, when the disciples saw the Master lifted up from the earth and carried on high, they were not seized by discouragement. Indeed, they experienced a great joy and felt driven to proclaim Christ's victory over death (see Mk 16:20). And the risen Lord worked with them, distributing to each a particular charism, so that the whole Christian community might reflect the harmonious richness of heaven.

St. Paul continues: "He gave gifts to men.... He gave some as apostles, others as prophets, others as evangelists, others as pastors and teachers … for building up the body of Christ.… to the extent of the full stature of Christ" (Eph 4:8, 11–13).

Dear friends, the Ascension tells us that in Christ our humanity is raised to the heights of God; thus, every time we pray, earth joins heaven. And like the smoke of burning incense lifts high its sweet odor, when we then raise up to the Lord our fervent and confident prayer in Christ, it passes through the heavens and reaches the throne of God. It is heard and answered by God.

MIDDAY REGINA CAELI, MAY 21, 2012

## MARY FOLLOWED HER SON TO HEAVEN

The Assumption of the Blessed Virgin Mary … impels us to lift our gaze to heaven: not to a heaven consisting of abstract ideas or even an imaginary heaven created by art, but the heaven of true reality which is God himself. God is heaven. He is our destination, the destination and the eternal dwelling place from which we come and for which we are striving.

St. Germanus, Bishop of Constantinople in the eighth century, in a homily given on the Feast of the Assumption, addressing the heavenly Mother of God, said: "You are the One who through your immaculate flesh reunited the Christian people with Christ.… Just as all who thirst hasten to the fountain, so every soul hastens to you, the Fountain of love, and as every man aspires to live, to see the light that never fades, so every Christian longs to enter the light of the Most Blessed Trinity where you already are."

It is these same sentiments that inspire us today as we contemplate Mary in God's glory. In fact, when she fell asleep in this world to reawaken in heaven, she simply followed her Son Jesus for the last time, on His longest and most crucial journey, His passage "from this world to the Father" (see Jn 13:1).

Like Him, together with Him, she departed this world to return "to the Father's house" (see Jn 14:2). And all this is not remote from us as it might seem at first sight, because we are all children of the Father, God. We are all brothers and sisters of Jesus, and we are all also children of Mary, our mother.

And we all aspire to happiness. And the happiness to which we all aspire is God, so we are all journeying on toward this happiness we call heaven which in reality is God. And Mary helps us; she encourages us to ensure that every moment of our life is a step forward on this exodus, on this journey toward God.

HOMILY, SOLEMNITY OF THE ASSUMPTION, AUGUST 15, 2008

## "GATE OF HEAVEN"

The new Eve followed the new Adam in suffering, in the passion, and so too in definitive joy. Christ is the first fruits, but His risen flesh is inseparable from that of His earthly mother, Mary. In Mary, all humanity is involved in the assumption to God, and together with her all creation, whose groans and sufferings, St. Paul tells us, are the birth-pangs of the new humanity.

Thus are born the new heaven and the new earth in which death shall be no more; neither shall there be mourning nor crying nor pain any more (see Rv 21:1–4).

What a great mystery of love is presented to us once again today for our contemplation! Christ triumphed over death with the omnipotence of His love. Love alone is omnipotent. This love impelled Christ to die for us and thus to overcome death. Yes, love alone gives access to the kingdom of life! And Mary entered after her Son, associated with His glory, after being associated with His passion.

She entered it with an uncontainable force, keeping the way behind her open to us all. And for this reason we invoke her today as "Gate of Heaven," "Queen of Angels," and "Refuge of Sinners." It is certainly not reasoning that will make us understand this reality which is so sublime, but rather simple, forthright faith and the silence of prayer that puts us in touch with the Mystery that infinitely exceeds us. Prayer helps us speak with God and hear how the Lord speaks to our heart.

Let us ask Mary today to make us the gift of her faith, that faith which enables us already to live in the dimension between finite and infinite, that faith which also transforms the sentiment of time and the passing of our existence, that faith in which we are profoundly aware that our life is not retracted by the past but attracted towards the future, towards God, where Christ, and behind Him Mary, has preceded us.

By looking at Mary's assumption into heaven we understand better that even though our daily life may be marked by trials and difficulties, it flows like a river to the divine ocean, to the fullness of joy and peace. We understand that our death is not the end but rather the entrance into life that knows no death. Our setting on the horizon of this world is our rising at the dawn of the new world, the dawn of the eternal day.

"Mary, while you accompany us in the toil of our daily living and dying, keep us constantly oriented to the true homeland of bliss. Help us to do as you did."

Homily, Solemnity of the Assumption, August 15, 2008

CHAPTER THIRTEEN

# And Is Seated at the Right Hand of God the Father Almighty

## "Sit at My Right Hand"

Psalm 110 … [was] very dear to the ancient Church and to believers of all times. This prayer may at first have been linked to the enthronement of a Davidic king. Yet its meaning exceeds the specific contingency of an historic event, opening to broader dimensions and thereby becoming a celebration of the victorious Messiah, glorified at God's right hand.

The Psalm begins with a solemn declaration: "The Lord says to my lord, 'Sit at my right hand, till I make your enemies your footstool'" (Ps 110:1).

God himself enthrones the king in glory, seating him at His right, a sign of very great honor and of absolute privilege. The king is thus admitted to sharing in the divine kingship, of which he is mediator to the people. The king's kingship is also brought into being in the victory over his adversaries whom God himself places at his feet. The victory over his enemies is the Lord's, but the king is enabled to share in it, and his triumph becomes a sign and testimony of divine power.

The royal glorification expressed at the beginning of the Psalm was adopted by the New Testament as a messianic prophecy. For this reason the verse is among those most frequently used by New Testament authors, either as an explicit quotation or as an allusion. With regard to the Messiah, Jesus himself mentioned this verse in order to show that the Messiah was greater than David, that He was David's Lord (see Mt 22:41–45; Mk 12:35–37; Lk 20:41–44).

Peter returned to it in his discourse at Pentecost, proclaiming that this enthronement of the king was brought about in the resurrection of Christ, and that Christ was henceforth seated at the right hand of the Father, sharing in God's kingship over the world (see Acts 2:29–35). Indeed, Christ is the enthroned Lord, the Son of Man seated at the right hand of God and coming on the clouds of heaven, as Jesus described himself during the trial before the Sanhedrin (see Mt 26:63–64; Mk 14:61–62; see also Lk 22:66–69).

He is the true King who, with the Resurrection, entered into glory at the right hand of the Father (see Rom 8:34; Eph 2:5; Col 3:1; Heb 8:1; 12:2), was made superior to angels, and seated in heaven above every power with every adversary at His feet, until the time when the last enemy, death, is to be defeated by Him once and for all (see 1 Cor 15:24–26; Eph 1:20–23; Heb 1:3–4; 2:5–8; 10:12–13; 1 Pet 3:22).

General Audience, November 16, 2011

## "Yours Is Princely Power"

We immediately understand that this King [described in Psalm 110], seated at the right hand of God, who shares in His kingship, is not one of those who succeeded David, but is actually the new David, the Son of God who triumphed over death and truly shares in God's glory. He is our King, who also gives us eternal life.

Hence an indissoluble relationship exists between the king celebrated by our Psalm and God. The two of them govern together as one, so that the psalmist can say that it is God himself who extends the sovereign's scepter, giving him the task of ruling over his adversaries, as verse 2 says: "The Lord sends forth from Zion your mighty scepter. Rule in the midst of your foes!"

The exercise of power is an office that the king receives directly from the Lord, a responsibility which he must exercise in dependence and obedience, thereby becoming a sign, within the people, of God's powerful and provident presence. Dominion over his foes, glory, and victory are gifts received that make the sovereign a mediator of the Lord's triumph over evil. He subjugates his enemies, transforming them; he wins them over with his love.

For this reason the king's greatness is celebrated in the following verse [according to the ancient Greek translation]: … "Yours is princely power in the day of your birth, in holy splendor; before the daystar, like the dew, I have begotten you."

This divine oracle concerning the king would thus assert a divine procreation, steeped in splendor and mystery, a secret and inscrutable origin linked to the arcane beauty of dawn and to the miracle of dew that sparkles in the fields in the early morning light and makes them fertile. In this way is outlined the figure of the king, indissolubly bound to the heavenly reality, who really comes from God, the Messiah who brings divine life to the people and is the mediator of holiness and salvation. Here too we see that all this is not achieved by the figure of a Davidic king but by the Lord Jesus Christ, who really comes from God; He is the light that brings divine life to the world.

General Audience, November 16, 2011

## The Priest-King

The first stanza of the [Messianic] Psalm [110] … is followed by another oracle, which unfolds a new perspective along the lines of a priestly dimension connected with kingship. Verse 4 says: "The Lord has sworn and will not change His mind, 'You are a priest for ever after the order of Melchizedek.'"

Melchizedek was the priest-king of Salem who had blessed Abraham and offered him bread and wine after the victorious military campaign the patriarch led to rescue his nephew Lot from the hands of enemies who had captured him (see Gen 14). Royal and priestly power converge in the figure of Melchizedek. They are then proclaimed by the Lord in a declaration that promises eternity: The King celebrated in the psalm will be a Priest forever, the mediator of the Lord's presence among His people, the intermediary of the blessing that comes from God who, in liturgical action, responds to it with the human answer of blessing.

The Letter to the Hebrews makes an explicit reference to this verse (see Heb 5:5–6, 10; 6:19–20), focusing on it the whole of chapter seven and developing its reflection on Christ's priesthood. Jesus, as the Letter to the Hebrews tells us in the light of Psalm 110, is the true and definitive priest who brings to fulfillment and perfects the features of Melchizedek's priesthood.

Melchizedek, as the Letter to the Hebrews says, was "without father or mother or genealogy" (v. 7:3a), hence not a priest according to the dynastic rules of Levitical priesthood. Consequently he "continues a priest for ever" (v. 7:3c), a prefiguration of Christ, the perfect High Priest who "has become a priest, not according to a legal requirement concerning bodily descent, but by the power of an indestructible life" (7:16).

In the risen Lord Jesus, who had ascended into heaven where He is seated at the right hand of the Father, the prophecy of our psalm is fulfilled, and the priesthood of Melchizedek is brought to completion. This is because, rendered absolute and eternal, it became a reality that never fades (see Heb 7:24).

The offering of bread and wine made by Melchizedek in Abraham's time is fulfilled in the Eucharistic action of Jesus, who offers himself in the bread and in the wine and, having conquered death, brings life to all believers. Since He is an eternal priest, "holy, blameless, unstained" (7:26), as the Letter to the Hebrews states further, "He is able for all time to save those who draw near to God through Him, since He always lives to make intercession for them" (7:25).

General Audience, November 16, 2011

## The Triumphant Sovereign

[In Psalm 110, a Messianic psalm], after the divine pronouncement in verse 4, with its solemn oath, the scene of the psalm changes and the poet, addressing the king directly, proclaims: "The Lord is at your right hand" (Ps 110:5a). If in verse 1 it was the king who was seated at God's right hand as a sign of supreme prestige and honor, the Lord now takes His place at the right of the sovereign to protect Him with this shield in battle and save Him from every peril. The king is safe, God is His champion, and they fight together and defeat every evil.

Thus the last verses of the psalm open with the vision of the triumphant sovereign. Supported by the Lord, having received both power and glory from Him (see v. 2), he opposes his foes, crushing his adversaries and judging the nations. The scene is painted in strong colors to signify the drama of the battle and the totality of the royal victory. The sovereign, protected by the Lord, demolishes every obstacle and moves ahead safely to victory.

He tells us: "Yes, there is widespread evil in the world. There is an ongoing battle between good and evil, and it seems as though evil were the stronger. But no, the Lord is stronger, Christ, our true King and Priest, for He fights with all God's power. In spite of all the things that make us doubt the positive outcome of history, Christ wins and good wins; love wins rather than hatred…."

The king of whom the Psalmist sang is definitively Christ, the Messiah who establishes the Kingdom of God and overcomes the powers of evil. He is the Word, begotten by the Father before every creature, before the dawn; the Son incarnate who died and rose and is seated in heaven; the eternal Priest who through the mystery of the bread and wine bestows forgiveness of sins and gives reconciliation with God; the King who lifts up his head, triumphing over death with His resurrection.

The paschal event of Christ thus becomes the reality to which the psalm invites us to look, to look at Christ to understand the meaning of true kingship, to live in service and in the gift of self, in a journey of obedience and love "to the end" (see Jn 13:1; 19:30).

In praying with this psalm, let us therefore ask the Lord to enable us to proceed on His paths, in the following of Christ, the Messiah King, ready to climb with Him the mount of the Cross to attain glory with Him, and to contemplate Him seated at the right hand of the Father, a victorious King and a merciful Priest who gives forgiveness and salvation to all men and women.

General Audience, November 16, 2011

## Mary Reigns with Christ

The Solemnity of the Assumption of the Blessed Virgin Mary, the oldest Marian feast, returns every year in the heart of summer. It is an opportunity to rise with Mary to the heights of the spirit, where one breathes the pure air of supernatural life and contemplates the most authentic beauty, the beauty of holiness. The atmosphere of today's celebration is steeped in paschal joy.

"Today," the antiphon of the Magnificat says, "the Virgin Mary was taken up to heaven. Rejoice, for she reigns with Christ forever. Alleluia."

This proclamation speaks to us of an event that is utterly unique and extraordinary, yet destined to fill the heart of every human being with hope and happiness. Mary is indeed the first fruit of the new humanity, the creature in whom the mystery of Christ — His incarnation, death, resurrection and ascension into heaven — has already fully taken effect, redeeming her from death and conveying her, body and soul, to the kingdom of immortal life.

For this reason, as the Second Vatican Council recalls, the Virgin Mary is a sign of certain hope and comfort to us (see *Lumen Gentium*, n. 68).

HOMILY, SOLEMNITY OF THE ASSUMPTION, AUGUST 15, 2008

CHAPTER FOURTEEN

# From There He Will Come to Judge the Living and the Dead

## Faith in Christ Looks Forward

At the conclusion of the central section of the Church's great *Credo* — the part that recounts the mystery of Christ, from His eternal birth of the Father and His temporal birth of the Virgin Mary, through His cross and resurrection to the Second Coming — we find the phrase: "He will come again in glory to judge the living and the dead."

From the earliest times, the prospect of the Judgment has influenced Christians in their daily living as a criterion by which to order their present life, as a summons to their conscience, and at the same time as hope in God's justice. Faith in Christ has never looked merely backwards or merely upwards, but always also forwards to the hour of justice that the Lord repeatedly proclaimed. This looking ahead has given Christianity its importance for the present moment.

In the arrangement of Christian sacred buildings, which were intended to make visible the historic and cosmic breadth of faith in Christ, it became customary to depict the Lord returning as a king — the symbol of hope — at the east end; while the west wall normally portrayed the Last Judgment as a symbol of our responsibility for our lives — a scene which followed and accompanied the faithful as they went out to resume their daily routine.

Encyclical Letter *Spe Salvi*, November 30, 2007, n. 41

## Essential Convictions About the Last Things

What are the basic convictions of Christians as regards the last things: death, the end of the world?

Their first conviction is the certainty that Jesus is risen, and is with the Father, and thus is with us forever. And no one is stronger than Christ, for He is with the Father; He is with us. We are consequently safe, free of fear....

Christ lives; He has overcome death; He has overcome all [evil powers that threaten us]. We live in this certainty, in this freedom, and in this joy. This is the first aspect of our living with regard to the future.

The second is the certainty that Christ is with me. And just as the future world in Christ has already begun, this also provides the certainty of hope. The future is not darkness in which no one can find his way. It is not like this.

Without Christ, even today the world's future is dark, and fear of the future is so common. Christians know that Christ's light is stronger, and therefore they live with a hope that is not vague, with a hope that gives them certainty and courage to face the future....

Their third conviction is that the Judge who returns — at the same time as Judge and Savior — has left us the duty to live in this world in accordance with His way of living. He has entrusted His talents to us. Our third conviction, therefore, is responsibility before Christ for the world, for our brethren and at the same time also for the certainty of His mercy. Both these things are important.

Since God can only be merciful we do not live as if good and evil were the same thing. This would be a deception. In reality, we live with a great responsibility. We have talents, and our responsibility is to work so that this world may be open to Christ, that it be renewed.

Yet even as we work responsibly, we realize that God is the true Judge. We are also certain that this Judge is good; we know His face, the face of the risen Christ, of Christ crucified for us. Therefore we can be certain of His goodness and advance with great courage.

General Audience, November 12, 2008

## Christ's Resurrection and Ours

The subject of the Resurrection … unfolds a new perspective, that of the expectation of the Lord's return. It thus brings us to ponder the relationship among the present time, the time of the Church and of the kingdom of Christ, and the future (*éschaton*) that lies in store for us, when Christ will consign the Kingdom to His Father (see 1 Cor 15:24).

Every Christian discussion of the last things, called eschatology, always starts with the event of the Resurrection; in this event the last things have already begun and, in a certain sense, are already present.

Very likely it was in the year 52 that St. Paul wrote the first of his letters, the First Letter to the Thessalonians, in which he speaks of this return of Jesus, called *parousia* or advent, His new, definitive, and manifest presence (see 1 Th 4:13–18).

The Apostle wrote these words to the Thessalonians, who were beset by doubts and problems: "For if we believe that Jesus died and rose, God will bring forth with Him from the dead those who have fallen asleep" (1 Th 4:14).

And Paul continues: "Those who have died in Christ will rise first. Then we, the living, the survivors, will be caught up with them in the clouds to meet the Lord in the air. Thenceforth we shall be with the Lord unceasingly" (1 Th 4:16–17).

Paul describes Christ's *parousia* in especially vivid tones and with symbolic imagery which, however, conveys a simple and profound message: We shall ultimately be with the Lord for ever. Over and above the images, this is the essential message: Our future is "to be with the Lord." As believers, we are already with the Lord in our lifetime; our future, eternal life, has already begun.

General Audience, November 12, 2008

## Our Responsibility in Light of Christ's Return

In his Second Letter to the Thessalonians, Paul … speaks of the negative incidents that must precede the final and conclusive event [of Christ's return to earth]. We must not let ourselves be deceived, he says, to think that, according to chronological calculations, the day of the Lord is truly imminent:

"On the question of the coming of our Lord Jesus Christ and our being gathered to Him, we beg you, brothers, not to be so easily agitated or terrified, whether by an oracular utterance, or rumor, or a letter alleged to be ours, into believing that the day of the Lord is here. Let no one seduce you, in any way" (2 Th 2:1–3).

The continuation of this text announces that before the Lord's arrival there will be apostasy, and one well described as the "man of lawlessness," "the son of perdition" (2 Th 2:3) must be revealed, whom tradition would come to call the Antichrist.

However, the intention of St. Paul's letter is primarily practical. He writes: "Indeed, when we were with you, we used to lay down the rule that whoever would not work, should not eat. We hear that some of you are unruly, not keeping busy but acting like busybodies. We enjoin all such and we urge them strongly in the Lord Jesus Christ, to earn the food they eat by working quietly" (2 Th 3:10–12).

In other words, the expectation of Jesus' *parousia* does not dispense us from working in this world but, on the contrary, creates responsibility to the divine Judge for our actions in this world. For this very reason our responsibility for working in and for this world increases.

We ... see the same thing ... in the Gospel [parable] of the talents, in which the Lord tells us that He has entrusted talents to everyone, and that the Judge will ask for an account of them, saying: "Have they been put to good use?" Hence the expectation of His return implies responsibility for this world.

General Audience, November 12, 2008

## Denial of Divine Judgment Leads to Presumption

In the modern era, the idea of the Last Judgment has faded into the background: Christian faith has been individualized and primarily oriented towards the salvation of the believer's own soul, while reflection on world history is largely dominated by the idea of progress. The fundamental content of awaiting a final judgment, however, has not disappeared; it has simply taken on a totally different form.

The atheism of the nineteenth and twentieth centuries is — in its origins and aims — a type of moralism, a protest against the injustices of the world and of world history. [It concludes that] a world marked by so much injustice, innocent suffering, and cynicism of power cannot be the work of a good God. A God with responsibility for such a world would not be a just God, much less a good God. It is for the sake of morality that this God has to be contested. Since there is no God to create justice, it seems man himself is now called to establish justice.

[Though] in the face of this world's suffering, protest against God is understandable, the claim that humanity can and must do what no God actually does or is able to do is both presumptuous and intrinsically false. It is no accident that this idea has led to the greatest forms of cruelty and violations of justice; rather, it is grounded in the intrinsic falsity of the claim.

A world which has to create its own justice is a world without hope. No one and nothing can answer for centuries of suffering. No one and nothing can guarantee that the cynicism of power — whatever beguiling ideological mask it adopts — will cease to dominate the world.

Encyclical Letter *Spe Salvi*, November 30, 2007, n. 42

## Justice Demands Eternal Life

In Him who was crucified … God now reveals His true face in the figure of the Sufferer who shares man's God-forsaken condition by taking it upon himself. This innocent Sufferer has attained the certitude of hope: There is a God, and God can create justice in a way that we cannot conceive, yet we can begin to grasp it through faith.

Yes, there is a resurrection of the flesh. There is justice. There is an "undoing" of past suffering, a reparation that sets things aright. For this reason, faith in the Last Judgment is first and foremost hope — the need for which was made abundantly clear in the upheavals of recent centuries.

I am convinced that the question of justice constitutes the essential argument, or in any case the strongest argument, in favor of faith in eternal life. The purely individual need for a fulfillment that is denied to us in this life, for an everlasting love that we await, is certainly an important motive for believing that man was made for eternity. But only in connection with the impossibility that the injustice of history should be the final word does the necessity for Christ's return and for new life become fully convincing.

To protest against God in the name of justice is not helpful. A world without God is a world without hope (see Eph 2:12). Only God can create justice. And faith gives us the certainty that He does so. The image of the Last Judgment is not primarily an image of terror, but an image of hope. For us it may even be the decisive image of hope.

Is it not also a frightening image? I would say: It is an image that evokes responsibility; an image, therefore, of that fear of which St. Hilary spoke when he said that all our fear has its place in love.

God is justice and creates justice. This is our consolation and our hope. And in His justice there is also grace. This we know by turning our gaze to the crucified and risen Christ.

Both these things — justice and grace — must be seen in their correct inner relationship. Grace does not cancel out justice. It does not make wrong into right. It is not a sponge which wipes everything away, so that whatever someone has done on earth ends up being of equal value.... Evildoers, in the end, do not sit at table at the eternal banquet beside their victims without distinction, as though nothing had happened.

Encyclical Letter *Spe Salvi,* November 30, 2007, n. 43–44

## Our Journey to Redemption

The divine blessing [that St. Paul expresses in Ephesians chapter 1] ends with the mention of the Holy Spirit who has been poured out into our hearts, the Paraclete whom we have received as a promised seal, "who is the guarantee of our inheritance until we acquire possession of it, to the praise of his glory" (Eph 1:14).

Redemption is not yet finished, as we know, but will reach its fulfillment when those whom God has ransomed are totally saved. We are still on the path of redemption, whose essential reality has been given with the death and resurrection of Jesus. We are on our way towards definitive redemption, towards the full liberation of God's children. And the Holy Spirit is the certainty that God will bring His plan of salvation to completion, when He will bring back to Christ, the only head, of "all things in heaven and on earth" (Eph 1:10).

St. John Chrysostom comments on this point: "God has chosen us for faith and has impressed in us the seal of the inheritance of future glory" (*Homilies on the Letter to the Ephesians 2, 11–14*). We must accept that the journey of redemption is also our journey, because God wants free creatures who freely say "yes"; but it is above all and first of all His journey. We are in His hands, and to walk in the way disclosed by Him is now our freedom. Let us walk on this path of redemption together with Christ and understand that redemption is [being] brought about.

General Audience, June 20, 2012

## God's Patience

How often we wish that God would show himself stronger, that He would strike decisively, defeating evil and creating a better world. All ideologies of power justify themselves in exactly this way: They justify the destruction of whatever would stand in the way of progress and the liberation of humanity.

We suffer on account of God's patience. And yet, we need His patience. God, who became a Lamb, tells us that the world is saved by the crucified One, not by those who crucified Him. The world is redeemed by the patience of God; it is destroyed by the impatience of man.

Homily, Papal Installation Mass, April 24, 2005

# CHAPTER FIFTEEN

# I Believe in the Holy Spirit

## Who Is the Holy Spirit?

Who or what is the Holy Spirit? How can we recognize Him? How do we go to Him and how does He come to us? What does He do?

The Church's great Pentecostal hymn — "*Veni, Creator Spiritus*" ("Come, Holy Spirit") — gives us a first answer. Here the hymn refers to the first verses of the Bible that describe the creation of the universe with recourse to images. The Bible says … that the Spirit of God was moving over the chaos, over the waters of the abyss.

Thus, we have discovered an initial answer to the question as to what the Holy Spirit is, what He does, and how we can recognize Him. He comes to meet us through creation and its beauty.…

However, in the course of human history, a thick layer of dirt has covered God's good creation, which makes it difficult if not impossible to perceive in it the Creator's reflection, although the knowledge of the Creator's existence is reawakened within us ever anew, as it were, spontaneously, at the sight of a sunset over the sea, on an excursion to the mountains, or before a flower that has just bloomed.

But the Creator Spirit comes to our aid. He has entered history and speaks to us in a new way. In Jesus Christ, God himself was made Man and allowed us, so to speak, to cast a glance at the intimacy of God himself.

And there we see something totally unexpected: In God, an "I" and a "You" exist. The mysterious God is not infinite loneliness; He is an event of love. If by gazing at creation we think we can glimpse the Creator Spirit — God himself, rather like creative mathematics, like a force that shapes the laws of the world and their order, but then, even, also like beauty — now we come to realize: The Creator Spirit has a heart. He is Love.

The Son who speaks to the Father exists, and They are both one in the Spirit, who constitutes, so to speak, the atmosphere of giving and loving which makes Them one God. This unity of love, which is God, is a unity far more sublime than could ever be even in the unity of the tiniest indivisible particle of matter. The Triune God himself is the one and only God.

Through Jesus let us, as it were, cast a glance at God in His intimacy. John, in his Gospel, expressed it like this: "No one has ever seen God; the only Son, who is in the bosom of the Father, He has made Him known" (Jn 1:18).

PRAYER VIGIL AND MEETING, PENTECOST, 2006

## THE SPIRIT DRAWS US TO GOD

Yet Jesus did not only let us see into God's intimacy; with Him, God also emerged, as it were, from His intimacy and came to meet us. This happened especially in His life, passion, death and resurrection, [and] in His words.

Jesus, however, is not content with coming to meet us. He wants more. He wants unification....

Not only must we know something about Him, but through Him we must be drawn to God. For this reason He had to die and be raised, since He is now no longer to be found in any specific place. But His Spirit, the Holy Spirit, emanates from Him and enters our hearts, thereby uniting us with Jesus himself and with the Father, the Triune God.

Pentecost is this: Jesus, and through Him, God himself, actually comes to us and draws us to himself. "He sends forth the Holy Spirit" — this is what Scripture says....

We find life in communion with the One who is life in person — in communion with the living God, a communion into which we are introduced by the Holy Spirit, who is called in the hymn of Vespers "*fons vivus*," a living source....

The Holy Spirit ... makes us sons and daughters of God. He involves us in the same responsibility that God has for His world, for the whole of humanity. He teaches us to look at the world, others, and ourselves with God's eyes. We do not do good as slaves who are not free to act otherwise, but we do it because we are personally responsible for the world; because we love truth and goodness, because we love God himself and, therefore, also His creatures. This is the true freedom to which the Holy Spirit wants to lead us.

Prayer Vigil and Meeting, Pentecost, 2006

## The Spirit Gives Unity

The Holy Spirit, in giving life and freedom, also gives unity. These are three gifts that are inseparable from one another....

To understand [unity], we might find a sentence useful which at first seems rather to distance us from it. Jesus said to Nicodemus, who came to Him with his questions by night: "The wind blow where it wills" (Jn 3:8). But the Spirit's will is not arbitrary. It is the will of truth and goodness.

Therefore, He does not blow from [just] anywhere, now from one place and then from another. His breath is not wasted, but brings us together because the truth unites and love unites.

The Holy Spirit is the Spirit of Jesus Christ, the Spirit who unites the Father with the Son in Love, which in the one God He gives and receives. He unites us so closely that St. Paul once said: "You are all one in Jesus Christ" (Gal 3:28).

With His breath, the Holy Spirit impels us towards Christ.

Prayer Vigil and Meeting, Pentecost, 2006

## The Spirit Inspires Missionary Zeal

The Holy Spirit desires unity; He desires totality. Therefore, His presence is finally shown above all in missionary zeal.

Anyone who has come across something true, beautiful, and good in his life — the one true treasure, the precious pearl — hastens to share it everywhere, in the family and at work, in all the contexts of his life.

He does so without any fear, because he knows he has received adoption as a son: without any presumption, for it is all a gift; without discouragement, for God's Spirit precedes His action in people's "hearts" and as a seed in the most diverse cultures and religions.

He does so without restraint, for He bears a piece of good news which is for all people and for all the peoples....

The Holy Spirit gives believers a superior vision of the world, of life, of history, and makes them custodians of the hope that never disappoints.

Let us pray to God the Father, therefore, through Our Lord Jesus Christ, in the grace of the Holy Spirit, so that the celebration of the Solemnity of Pentecost may be like an ardent flame and a blustering wind for Christian life and for the mission of the whole Church.

Prayer Vigil and Meeting, Pentecost, 2006

## Remaining Close to the Spirit

In daily life … it is … difficult in practice to perceive the action of the Holy Spirit, or even to be personally a means to enable Him to be present, to ensure the presence of that Breath which sweeps away the prejudices of time, which creates light in the darkness and makes us feel not only that faith has a future but that it is the future.

How can we do this? We cannot of course do it on our own. In the end, it is the Lord who helps us. But we must be available as instruments.

I would say simply: No one can give what he does not personally possess. In other words, we cannot pass on the Holy Spirit effectively or make Him perceptible to others unless we ourselves are close to Him.

This is why I think that the most important thing is that we ourselves remain, so to speak, within the radius of the Holy Spirit's breath, in contact with Him. Only if we are continually touched within by the Holy Spirit, if He dwells in us, will it be possible for us to pass Him on to others.

Then He gives us the imagination and creative ideas about how to act, ideas that cannot be planned but are born from the situation itself, because it is there that the Holy Spirit is at work. Thus,… we ourselves must remain within the radius of the Holy Spirit's breath.

Q&A with Bolzano-Bressanone Clergy,
Bressanone, Italy, August 6, 2008

## Life with Christ in the Spirit

John's Gospel tell us that after the Resurrection, the Lord went to His disciples, breathed upon them, and said: "Receive the Holy Spirit" [Jn 20:22]. This is a parallel to Genesis, where God breathes on the mixture He made with the dust from the earth, and it comes to life and becomes man.

Then man, who is inwardly darkened and half dead, receives Christ's breath anew, and it is this Breath of God that gives his life a new dimension, that gives him life with the Holy Spirit.

We can say, therefore, that the Holy Spirit is the breath of Jesus Christ; and we, in a certain sense, must ask Christ to breathe on us always, so that His breath will become alive and strong and work upon the world. This means that we must keep close to Christ.

We do so by meditating on his Word. We know that the principal author of the Sacred Scriptures is the Holy Spirit. When through His Word we speak with God, when we do not only seek the past in it but truly the Lord who is present and speaks to us, then … it is as if we were to find ourselves strolling in the garden of the Holy Spirit; we talk to Him, and He talks to us.

Here, learning to be at home in this environment, in the environment of the Word of God, is a very important thing which, in a certain sense, introduces us into the breath of God. And then, naturally, this listening, walking in the environment of the Word must be transformed into a response, a response in prayer, in contact with Christ.

And of course, [we encounter the Spirit] first of all in the Blessed Sacrament of the Eucharist in which He comes to us and enters us and is, as it were, amalgamated with us. Then, however, also in the Sacrament of Penance, which always purifies us, which washes away the grime that daily life deposits in us.

In short, it is a life with Christ in the Holy Spirit, in the Word of God, and in the communion of the Church, in her community. St. Augustine said: "If you desire the Spirit of God, you must be in the Body of Christ." Christ's Spirit moves within the Mystical Body of Christ.

All this must determine the shape that our day takes in such a way that it becomes structured, a day in which God has access to us all the time, in which we are in continuous contact with Christ and in which, for this very reason, we are continuously receiving the breath of the Holy Spirit.

Q&A WITH BOLZANO-BRESSANONE CLERGY,
BRESSANONE, ITALY, AUGUST 6, 2008

## THE SPIRIT AND THE CHURCH

The inseparability of Christ and the Holy Spirit … is perhaps most beautifully seen in St. John's account of the risen Christ's first appearance to the disciples. The Lord breathes on His disciples, and thus bestows the Holy Spirit upon them.

The Holy Spirit is the breath of Christ. And just as the breath of God on the morning of Creation changed the dust of the earth into a living man, so the breath of Christ admits us to … communion with the Son, making us a new creation. Hence it is the Holy Spirit who prompts us to say together: "Abba! Father!" (see Jn 20:22; Rom 8:15).

The link between Spirit and Church thus naturally emerges.… In his First Letter to the Corinthians, chapter 12, and in his Letter to the Romans, chapter 12, Paul described the Church as the Body of Christ, and thus as an organism of the Holy Spirit, in which the gifts of the Holy Spirit fuse individuals into a single living whole.

The Holy Spirit is the Spirit of the Body of Christ. In the fullness of this Body we discover our task, we live for one another and in dependence on others, drawing deep life from the One who lived and suffered for us all and who, through His Spirit, draws us to himself in the unity of all God's children. As Augustine says in this regard: "Do you too desire to live from the Spirit of Christ? Then be in the Body of Christ" (*Tract. in Jo.* 26, 13).

Thus, with the theme of the Holy Spirit ... the whole breadth of the Christian faith becomes visible.

Address to the Roman Curia, December 22, 2008

## Babel and Pentecost

The account of Pentecost in the Acts of the Apostles ... (see Acts 2:1–11), has in its background one of the last great frescos that we find at the beginning of the Old Testament: the ancient story of the construction of the Tower of Babel (see Gen 11:1–9). But what is Babel?

It is the description of a kingdom in which men have concentrated so much power that they think that they no longer need a distant God. And they believe that they are strong enough to build a way to heaven by themselves and open its gates to put themselves in God's place.

But precisely in this situation something strange and unique occurs. While the men were working to build the tower, suddenly they realized that they were working against each other. While they tried to be like God, they ran the risk of no longer even being men, because they lost a fundamental element of being human persons: the capacity to agree, to understand, and to work together.

This biblical account contains a perennial truth. We can see it throughout history, but in our world too. With the progress of science and technology we have developed the power to dominate forces of nature, to manipulate the elements, to manufacture living beings, almost attaining the ability to make human beings.

In this context, praying to God seems like something obsolete, useless, because we can build and realize anything we want. But we do not grasp that we are reliving the very experience of Babel.

Indeed, we have multiplied the possibilities of communicating, of having information, of transmitting news; but can we say that the capacity to understand each other has grown? Or is it perhaps the case that, paradoxically, we understand each other less and less? Have not a sense of diffidence, of suspicion, of mutual fear worked themselves into our lives to the point that we have become dangerous to each other?…

Can unity, concord really exist? How can they exist?

We find the answer in Sacred Scripture: Only with the gift of God's Spirit can there be unity. This Spirit will give us a new heart and a new tongue, a new capacity to communicate. And this is what happened on Pentecost.

On that morning, fifty days after Easter, a tempestuous wind blew upon Jerusalem, and the flame of the Holy Spirit descended upon the disciples, who were gathered together, settling on each and lighting divine fire in them, a fire of love with the power to transform. The fear dissipated, the heart felt a new force, tongues were loosened and began to speak with boldness, in such a way that all could understand the proclamation of Jesus Christ dead and risen. At Pentecost, where there was division and estrangement, unity and understanding were born.

HOMILY, SOLEMNITY OF PENTECOST, JUNE 12, 2011

## The Spirit of Unity and Truth

Jesus says: "When He comes, the Spirit of truth, He will guide you to all truth" (Jn 16:13). Here Jesus, speaking of the Holy Spirit, explains to us what the Church is and how she must live to be herself, to be the place of unity and of communion in the Truth.

He tells us that acting like Christians means not being shut up in our own "I," but relating ourselves to the whole. It means welcoming the whole Church into us or, better, letting ourselves be interiorly taken up into her. So when I speak, think, act as a Christian, I do not do this closing myself in my "I." I always do it within the whole and from the whole.

Thus the Holy Spirit, the Spirit of unity and truth, can continue to resound in our hearts and in the minds of men and move them to engage with and welcome each other. The Spirit, precisely because He acts in this way, leads us to the whole truth, which is Jesus himself, brings us to fathom and understand it. We do not grow in knowledge [by] closing ourselves up in our "I," but only in becoming capable of listening and sharing in the "we" of the Church, with an attitude of profound interior humility.

And thus it becomes clear why Babel is Babel and Pentecost is Pentecost. Where men want to make themselves God, they can only oppose each other. Where they place themselves in the Lord's truth instead, they open up to the action of the Spirit, who sustains and unites them.

Homily, Solemnity of Pentecost, June 12, 2011

## The Spirit Brings Unity to the Soul

The Apostle says: "Walk according to the Spirit and do not gratify the desires of the flesh" (Gal 5:16). St. Paul explains to us that our personal life is marked by an interior conflict, by division, between impulses that come from the flesh and those that come from the Spirit; and we cannot . of them.

We cannot, in fact, be simultaneously egoistic and generous, giving in to the temptation to dominate others and experiencing the joy of disinterested service. We must choose which impulse to follow, and we can do it authentically only with the help of the Spirit of Christ.

St. Paul lists … the works of the flesh (see Gal 5:19–21). They are the sins of egoism and violence, such as strife, discord, jealousy, dissension. They are thoughts and deeds that to not allow us to live in a truly human and Christian way, in love. The latter is a direction that leads to the losing of one's own life.

The Holy Spirit leads us toward the heights of God, that we might already live on this earth from the seed of divine life that is in us. St. Paul, in fact, states: "The fruit of the Spirit is love, joy, peace" (Gal 5:22). And let us note that the Apostle uses the plural to describe the works of the flesh, which divide and scatter us, while he uses the singular to define the Spirit's action — He speaks of "fruit" — just as the scattering of Babel is opposed to the unity of Pentecost.

Dear friends, we must live according to the Spirit of unity and of truth, and for this we must pray that the Spirit enlighten us and lead us to overcome the fascination with following our own truths and [follow] instead the truth of Christ transmitted in the Church.

HOMILY, SOLEMNITY OF PENTECOST, JUNE 12, 2011

CHAPTER SIXTEEN

# The Holy Catholic Church

## One, Holy, Catholic, and Apostolic

[T]he Church was catholic from the very outset … her universality is not the result of the successive inclusion of various communities. Indeed, from the first moment [at Pentecost], the Holy Spirit created her as the Church of all peoples. She embraces the whole world; surmounts all distinctions of race, class and nation; tears down all barriers; and brings people together in the profession of the triune God.

Since the beginning the Church has been one, catholic, and apostolic: This is her true nature and must be recognized as such. She is not holy because of her members' ability, but because God himself, with His Spirit, never ceases to create her, purify her and sanctify her.

Homily, Solemnity of Pentecost, June 12, 2011

## The Meaning of the Church's Catholicity

The Feast of the Holy Apostles Peter and Paul is at the same time a grateful memorial of the great witnesses of Jesus Christ and a solemn confession for the Church: *one, holy, catholic and apostolic*. It is first and foremost a feast of catholicity. The sign of Pentecost — the new community that speaks all languages and unites all peoples into one people, in one family of God — this sign has become a reality. Our liturgical assembly, at which bishops are gathered from all parts of the world, people of many cultures and nations, is an image of the family of the Church distributed throughout the earth.

Strangers have become friends; crossing every border, we recognize one another as brothers and sisters. This brings to fulfillment the mission of St. Paul, who knew that he was the "minister of Christ Jesus among the Gentiles, with the priestly duty of preaching the Gospel of God so that the Gentiles [might] be offered up as a pleasing sacrifice, consecrated by the Holy Spirit" (Rom 15:16).

The purpose of the mission is that humanity itself becomes a living glorification of God, the true worship that God expects. This is the deepest meaning of *catholicity* — a *catholicity* that has already been given to us, towards which we must constantly start out again. *Catholicity* does not only express a horizontal dimension, the gathering of many people in unity, but also a vertical dimension. It is only by raising our eyes to God, by opening ourselves to Him, that we can truly become one.

Eucharistic Concelebration, Solemnity of Saints Peter and Paul, June 29, 2005

## The Bond Between the Church's Catholicity and Unity

*Catholicity* means *universality* — a multiplicity that becomes unity; a unity that nevertheless remains multiplicity.... In the second century, the founder of Catholic theology, St. Irenaeus of Lyons, described very beautifully this bond between catholicity and unity, and I quote him. He says:

"The Church spread across the world diligently safeguards this doctrine and this faith, forming as it were one family: the same faith, with one mind and one heart, the same preaching, teaching, and tradition as if she had but one mouth. Languages abound according to the region, but the power of our tradition is one and the same.

"The Churches in Germany do not differ in faith or tradition, neither do those in Spain, Gaul, Egypt, Libya, the Orient, the center of the earth. Just as the sun, God's creature, is one alone and identical throughout the world, so the light of true preaching shines everywhere and illuminates all who desire to attain knowledge of the truth" (*Adv. Haer.* I 10, 2).

The *unity* of men and women in their multiplicity has become possible because God, this one God of heaven and earth, has shown himself to us; because the essential truth about our lives, our "where from?" and "where to?" became visible when He revealed himself to us and enabled us to see His face, himself, in Jesus Christ.

This truth about the essence of our being, living, and dying — a truth that God made visible — unites us and makes us brothers and sisters. *Catholicity* and *unity* go hand in hand. And *unity* has a content: the faith that the Apostles passed on to us in Christ's name.

Eucharistic Concelebration, Solemnity of Saints Peter and Paul, June 29, 2005

## The Meaning of Apostolicity

We have said that the *catholicity* of the Church and the *unity* of the Church go together. The fact that both dimensions become visible to us in the figures of the holy Apostles already shows us the consequent characteristic of the Church: She is *apostolic*. What does this mean?

The Lord established twelve apostles, just as the sons of Jacob were twelve. By so doing, He was presenting them as leaders of the People of God which — henceforth universal — from that time has included all the peoples.

St. Mark tells us that Jesus called the Apostles so "to be with Him, and to be sent out" (Mk 3:14). This seems almost a contradiction in terms. We would say: "Either they stayed with Him, or they were sent forth and set out on their travels."

Pope St. Gregory the Great says a word about angels that helps us resolve this contradiction. He says that angels are always sent out, and at the same time are always in God's presence, and continues, "Wherever they are sent, wherever they go, they always journey on in God's heart" (*Homily*, 34,13).

The Book of Revelation described bishops as "angels" in their Church, so we can state: The Apostles and their successors must always be with the Lord and precisely in this way: Wherever they may go, they must always be in communion with Him and live by this communion.

The Church is apostolic because she professes the faith of the Apostles and attempts to live it. There is a unity that marks the Twelve called by the Lord, but there is also continuity in the apostolic mission.

St. Peter, in his First Letter, described himself as "a fellow elder" of the presbyters to whom he writes (1 Pt 5:1). And with this he expressed the principle of apostolic succession: The same ministry which he had received from the Lord now continues in the Church through priestly ordination. The Word of God is not only written, but — thanks to the testimonies that the Lord in the sacrament has inscribed in the apostolic ministry — it remains a living word....

*Unity* as well as *apostolicity* are bound to the Petrine service that visibly unites the Church of all places and all times, thereby preventing each one of us from slipping into the kind of false autonomy that all too easily becomes particularization of the Church and might consequently jeopardize her independence. So let us not forget that the purpose of all offices and ministries is basically that "we [all] become one in faith and in the knowledge of God's son, and form that perfect man who is Christ come to full stature," so that the Body of Christ may grow and "build itself up in love" (Eph 4:13, 16)....

Let us implore the Lord with all our hearts to guide us to full *unity* so that the splendor of the truth, which alone can create *unity*, may once again become visible in the world.

Eucharistic Concelebration, Solemnity of Saints Peter and Paul, June 29, 2005

## The Church's Holiness Comes from God

Today's Gospel tells of the profession of faith of St. Peter, on whom the Church was founded: "You are the Messiah ... the Son of the living God" (Mt 16:16). Having spoken ... of the Church as *one, catholic and apostolic* but not yet of the Church as *holy*, let us now recall another profession of Peter: His response on behalf of the Twelve at the moment when so many abandoned Christ. "We have come to believe; we are convinced that you are God's holy one" (Jn 6:69). What does this mean?

Jesus, in His great priestly prayer, says that He is consecrating himself for His disciples, an allusion to the sacrifice of His death (see Jn 17:19). By saying this, Jesus implicitly expresses His role as the true High Priest who brings about the mystery of the "Day of Reconciliation," no longer only in substitutive rites but in the concrete substance of His own Body and Blood.

The Old Testament term "the Holy One of the Lord" identified Aaron as the High Priest who had the task of bringing about Israel's sanctification (see Ps 106:16; Vulgate: Sir 45:6). Peter's profession of Christ, whom he declares to be the Holy One of God, fits into the context of the Eucharistic discourse in which Jesus announces the Day of Reconciliation through the sacrificial offering of himself: "The bread I will give is My flesh, for the life of the world" (Jn 6:51).

So this profession is the background of the priestly mystery of Jesus, His sacrifice for us all. The Church is not *holy* by herself; in fact, she is made up of sinners — we all know this, and it is plain for all to see. Rather, she is made holy ever anew by the Holy One of God, by the purifying love of Christ.

God did not only speak, but loved us very realistically; He loved us to the point of the death of His own Son. It is precisely here that we are shown the full grandeur of revelation that has, as it were, inflicted wounds in the heart of God himself. Then each one of us can say personally, together with St. Paul, I live "a life of faith in the Son of God, who loved me and gave himself for me" (Gal 2:20).

Let us pray to the Lord that the truth of these words may be deeply impressed in our hearts, together with his joy and with his responsibility. Let us pray that, shining out from the Eucharistic celebration, it will become increasingly the force that shapes our lives.

Eucharistic Concelebration, Solemnity of Saints
Peter and Paul, St. Peter's Basilica, June 29, 2005

## The Church of God

"The Church of God" (1 Cor 1:2) is not only a collection of various local Churches.... These various local Churches ... make up one Church of God. All together they are "the Church of God" which precedes the individual local Churches and is expressed or brought into being in them.

It is important to observe that the word "Church" almost always appears with the additional qualification "of

God." She is not a human association, born from ideas or common interests, but a convocation of God. He has convoked her; thus, in all her manifestations she is one. The oneness of God creates the oneness of the Church in all the places in which she is found....

The Church ... is not ours: The Church is the Body of Christ, it is a "Church *of God*," "God's field, God's building ... God's temple" (1 Cor 3:9, 16)....

The Apostle [Paul] helps us to understand ever more deeply the mystery of the Church in her different dimensions as an assembly of God in the world. This is the greatness of the Church and the greatness of our call: We are a temple of God in the world, a place in which God truly dwells, and at the same time we are a community, a family of God who is love.

As a family and home of God, we must practice God's love in the world, and thus, with the power that comes from faith, be a place and a sign of His presence.

Let us pray the Lord to grant us to be increasingly His Church, His Body, the place where His love is present in this world of ours and in our history.

General Audience, October 15, 2008

## Unity and Diversity

The Holy Spirit acts corporeally; He does not act only subjectively or "spiritually." The risen Christ said to His disciples, who supposed that they were seeing only a "spirit": "It is I myself; touch me, and see; for a spirit has not flesh and bones as you see that I have" (Lk 24:39).

This applies for the risen Christ in every period of history. The risen Christ is not a ghost; He is not merely a spirit, a thought, only an idea.

He has remained incarnate — it is the risen One who took on our flesh — and always continues to build His Body, making it His Body. The Spirit breathes where He wills, and His will is unity embodied, a unity that encounters the world and transforms it.

In his Letter to the Ephesians, St. Paul tells us that this Body of Christ, which is the Church, has joints (Eph 4:16) and even names them: They are apostles, prophets, evangelists, pastors and teachers (see 4:12). In His gifts, the Spirit is multifaceted — we see it here. If we look at history,... then we realize that He inspires ever-new gifts; we see how different are the bodies that He creates and how He works bodily ever anew.

But in Him, multiplicity and unity go hand in hand. He breathes where He wills. He does so unexpectedly, in unexpected places and in ways previously unheard of. And with what diversity and corporality does He do so! And it is precisely here that diversity and unity are inseparable....

The Spirit blows where He wills. But His will is unity. He leads us towards Christ through his Body.

"From Christ," St. Paul tells us, "the whole body, joined and knit together by every joint with which it is supplied, when each part is working properly, makes bodily growth and upbuilds itself in love" (Eph 4:16).

Prayer Vigil and Meeting, Pentecost, 2006

## No One Becomes a Christian Alone

In the sixth chapter of the Letter to the Romans, St. Paul speaks of Baptism in a very profound way.... "Do you not know that all of us who have been baptized into Christ Jesus were baptized into His death? We were buried therefore with

Him by Baptism into death, so that as Christ was raised from the dead by the glory of the Father, we too might walk in newness of life" (Rom 6:3–4)….

"We have been baptized" is a passive. No one can baptize himself; he needs the other. No one can become Christian on his own. Becoming Christian is a passive process. Only by another can we be made Christians, and this "other" who makes us Christians, who gives us the gift of faith, is in the first instance the community of believers, the Church.

From the Church we receive faith, Baptism. Unless we let ourselves be formed by this community we do not become Christians. An autonomous, self-produced Christianity is a contradiction in itself.

In the first instance, this "other" is the community of believers, the Church. Yet in the second instance, this community does not act on its own, either, according to its own ideas and desires. The community also lives in the same passive process: Christ alone can constitute the Church. Christ is the true giver of the sacraments.

General Audience, December 10, 2008

## The Eucharist and the Church

The Eucharist makes constantly present the risen Christ who continues to give himself to us, calling us to participate in the banquet of His Body and His Blood. From full communion with Him flows every other element of the Church's life: first of all, communion among all the faithful, the commitment to proclaiming and witnessing to the Gospel, the ardor of love for all, especially the poorest and lowliest.

Striving to Be the *Servus Servorum Dei,* April 20, 2005

## In Receiving Christ's Body, We Become One Body

St. Paul says: "The cup of blessing which we bless, is it not a participation in the Blood of Christ? The bread which we break, is it not a participation in the Body of Christ? Because there is one bread, we who are many are one body, for we all partake of the one bread" (1 Cor 10:16–17)

In these words the personal and social character of the sacrament of the Eucharist … appears. Christ personally unites himself with each one of us, but Christ himself is also united with the man and the woman who are next to me. And the bread is for me but it is also for the other.

Thus Christ unites all of us with himself and all of us with one another. In communion we receive Christ. But Christ is likewise united with my neighbor: Christ and my neighbor are inseparable in the Eucharist. And thus we are all one bread and one body.

A Eucharist without solidarity with others is a Eucharist abused. And here we come to the root and, at the same time, the kernel of the doctrine on the Church as the Body of Christ, of the risen Christ.

We also perceive the full realism of this doctrine. Christ gives us His Body in the Eucharist; He gives himself in His Body and thus makes us His Body; He unites us with His risen Body.

If man eats ordinary bread, in the digestive process this bread becomes part of his body, transformed into a substance of human life. But in Holy Communion the inverse process is brought about. Christ, the Lord, assimilates us into himself, introducing us into His glorious Body, and thus we all become His Body.

General Audience, December 10, 2008

## The Church Militant

Today the word *ecclesia militans* ["the Church Militant"] is somewhat out of fashion. But in reality we can understand ever better that it is true, that it bears truth in itself.

We see how evil wishes to dominate the world, and that it is necessary to enter into battle with evil. We see how it does so in so many ways, bloody, with the different forms of violence, but also masked with goodness, and precisely this way destroying the moral foundations of society.

St. Augustine said that the whole of history is a struggle between two loves: love of oneself to contempt of God; love of God to contempt of self, in martyrdom. We are in this struggle.

Papal Greeting to the Cardinals, May 22, 2012

## The Law of the Church Frees Us

The Church … recognizes in her laws the nature as well as the means and pastoral function for pursuing her own end, which — as is well known — is the achievement of the *salus animarum,* the salvation of souls.…

Since canon law outlines the rules necessary for the People of God to orient themselves effectively to their own end, one understands how important it is that this law be loved and observed by all the faithful.… Church law is first and foremost *lex libertatis*: a law that sets us free to adhere to Jesus.

Address to the Study Congress of the Pontifical Council for Legislative Texts, January 25, 2008

## The Role of Peter's Successors

When we read the saints' names, we can see how often they have been — and continue to be — first and foremost simple people from whom shone — and shines — a radiant light that can lead others to Christ.

But this chorus of witnesses is also endowed with a clearly defined structure: the successors of the Apostles, the bishops, who are publicly responsible for ensuring that the network of these witnesses survives. The power and grace required for this service are conferred upon bishops through the sacrament of episcopal ordination. In this network of witnesses, the Successor of Peter has a special task. It was Peter who, on the Apostles' behalf, made the first profession of faith: "You are the Messiah, the Son of the living God" (Mt 16:16).

This is the task of all Peter's Successors: to be the guide in the profession of faith in Christ, Son of the living God. The Chair of Rome is above all the Seat of this belief. From high up on this Chair, the Bishop of Rome is constantly bound to repeat: *Dominus Iesus* — "Jesus is Lord," as Paul wrote in his letters to the Romans (Rom 10:9) and to the Corinthians (1 Cor 12:3). To the Corinthians he stressed: "Even though there are so-called gods in the heavens and on the earth … for us there is one God, the Father … and one Lord Jesus Christ, through whom everything was made and through whom we live" (1 Cor 8:5).

The Chair of Peter obliges all who hold it to say, as Peter said during a crisis time among the disciples when so many wanted to leave Him: "Lord, to whom shall we go? You have the words of eternal life. We have come to believe; we are convinced that you are God's holy one" (Jn 6:68ff).

The One who sits on the Chair of Peter must remember the Lord's words to Simon Peter at the Last Supper: "You in turn must strengthen your brothers" (Lk 22:32). The one who holds the office of the Petrine ministry must be aware that he is a frail and weak human being — just as his own powers are frail and weak — and is constantly in need of purification and conversion.

But he can also be aware that the power to strengthen his brethren in the faith and keep them united in the confession of the crucified and risen Christ comes from the Lord. In St. Paul's First Letter to the Corinthians, we find the oldest account we have of the Resurrection. Paul faithfully received it from the witnesses.

This account first speaks of Christ's death for our sins, of His burial and of His resurrection that took place the third day; and then says: "[Christ] was seen by Cephas [Peter], then by the Twelve" (1 Cor 15:4). Thus the importance of the mandate conferred upon Peter to the end of time is summed up: being a witness of the risen Christ.

Homily, Mass of Possession of the Chair, May 7, 2005

## Sacred Scripture and the Church

The Bishop of Rome sits upon the Chair [of Peter] to bear witness to Christ. Thus, the Chair is the symbol of the *potestas docendi*, the power to teach that is an essential part of the mandate of binding and loosing which the Lord conferred on Peter, and after him, on the Twelve (see Mt 16:18–19; 18:18).

In the Church, Sacred Scripture, the understanding of which increases under the inspiration of the Holy Spirit, and the ministry of its authentic interpretation that was conferred upon the Apostles, are indissolubly bound. Whenever Sacred Scripture is separated from the living voice of the Church, it falls prey to disputes among experts.

Of course, all they have to tell us is important and invaluable. The work of scholars is a considerable help in understanding the living process in which the Scriptures developed, hence, also in grasping their historical richness.

Yet science alone cannot provide us with a definitive and binding interpretation. It is unable to offer us, in its interpretation, that certainty with which we can live and for which we can even die. A greater mandate is necessary for this, which cannot derive from human abilities alone. The voice of the living Church is essential for this, of the Church entrusted until the end of time to Peter and to the College of the Apostles.

This power of teaching frightens many people in and outside the Church. They wonder whether freedom of conscience is threatened or whether it is a presumption opposed to freedom of thought. It is not like this.

The power that Christ conferred upon Peter and his Successors is, in an absolute sense, a mandate to serve. The power of teaching in the Church involves a commitment to the service of obedience to the faith. The Pope is not an absolute monarch whose thoughts and desires are law. On the contrary: The Pope's ministry is a guarantee of obedience to Christ and to his Word. He must not proclaim his own ideas, but rather constantly bind himself and the Church to obedience to God's Word, in the face of every attempt to adapt it or water it down, and every form of opportunism.…

The Pope knows that in his important decisions, he is bound to the great community of faith of all times, to the binding interpretations that have developed throughout the Church's pilgrimage. Thus, his power is not being above, but [rather] at the service of, the Word of God. It is incumbent upon him to ensure that this Word continues to be present in its greatness and to resound in its purity, so that it is not torn to pieces by continuous changes in usage.

The Chair is — let us say it again — a symbol of the power of teaching, which is a power of obedience and service, so that the Word of God — the truth! — may shine out among us and show us the way of life.

Homily, Mass of Possession of the Chair, May 7, 2005

## Mary and the Church

The presence of the Mother of God with the Eleven after the Ascension [see Acts 1:12–14] is not a mere historical annotation of something of the past. Rather, it acquires a significance of great value, for she shares what is most precious to them: the living memory of Jesus in prayer; and she shares this mission of Jesus: to preserve the memory of Jesus and thereby to preserve his presence....

From the Ascension of the risen One to the first Christian Pentecost, the Apostles and the Church gathered with Mary to await with her the gift of the Holy Spirit, without whom they could not become witnesses. She who has already received Him, in order to conceive the Incarnate Word, shares with the whole Church the expectation of the same gift so that "Christ may be formed" (Gal 4:19) in every believer's heart.

If there is no Church without Pentecost, without the Mother of Jesus there is no Pentecost either, since she lived in a singular way what the Church experiences each day under the action of the Holy Spirit. St. Chromatius of Aquileia comments in these words on the annotation in the Acts of the Apostles: "So the Church had gathered in the upper room together with Mary, the Mother of Jesus, and with his brethren. It is therefore impossible to speak of the Church if Mary, Mother of the Lord, is not present.... The Church of

Christ is wherever the Incarnation of Christ by the Virgin is preached, and wherever the Apostles, who are the Lord's brethren, preach, it is there that the Gospel is heard (*Sermo* 30, 1: *SC* 164, 135).

General Audience, March 14, 2012

CHAPTER SEVENTEEN

# The Communion of Saints

## We Are Not Alone

I am not alone. I do not have to carry alone what in truth I could never carry alone. All the saints of God are there to protect me, to sustain me and to carry me. And your prayers, my dear friends, your indulgence, your love, your faith, and your hope accompany me.

Indeed, the communion of saints consists not only of the great men and women who went before us and whose names we know. All of us belong to the communion of saints: We who have been baptized in the name of the Father, and of the Son, and of the Holy Spirit; we who draw life from the gift of Christ's Body and Blood, through which He transforms us and makes us like himself.

Homily, Papal Installation Mass, April 24, 2005

## Everyday Saints

During the liturgical year, the Church invites us to commemorate a host of saints, the ones, that is, who lived charity to the full, who knew how to love and follow Christ in their daily lives. They tell us that it is possible for everyone to take this road. In every epoch of the Church's history, in every latitude of the world map, the saints belong to all the ages and to every state of life. They are actual faces of every people, language, and nation. And they have very different characters.

Actually, I must say that also for my personal faith, many saints, not all, are true stars in the firmament of history. And I would like to add that for me not only a few great saints whom I love and whom I know well are "signposts," but precisely also the simple saints — that is, the good people I see in my life who will never be canonized.

They are ordinary people, so to speak, without visible heroism. But in their everyday goodness I see the truth of faith. This goodness, which they have developed in the faith of the Church, is for me the most reliable apology of Christianity and the sign of where the truth lies.

General Audience, April 13, 2011

## All Called to Holiness

In the communion of saints, canonized and not canonized, the Church gives thanks to Christ in all her members. We enjoy their presence and their company and cultivate the firm hope that we shall be able to imitate their journey and share one day in the same blessed life, eternal life.

Dear friends, how great and beautiful, as well as simple, is the Christian vocation seen in this light! We are all called to holiness: It is the very measure of Christian living. Once again St. Paul expresses it with great intensity when he writes:

"Grace was given to each of us according to the measure of Christ's gift.... His gifts were that some should be apostles, some prophets, some evangelists, some pastors and teachers, to equip the saints for the work of ministry, for building up the body of Christ, until we all attain to the unity of the faith and of the knowledge of the Son of God, to mature manhood, to the measure of the stature of the fullness of Christ" (Eph 4:7, 11–13).

I would like to ask all to open themselves to the action of the Holy Spirit, who transforms our life, to be as small pieces in the great mosaic of holiness that God continues to create in history, so that the face of Christ may shine out in the fullness of its splendor. Let us not be afraid to aim high, for God's heights; let us not be afraid that God will ask too much of us, but let ourselves be guided by His Word in every daily action, even when we feel poor, inadequate, sinners. It will be He who transforms us in accordance with His love.

General Audience, April 13, 2011

## Celebrating the Saints

Our Eucharistic celebration [on All Saints' Day] began with the exhortation: "Let us all rejoice in the Lord." The liturgy invites us to share in the heavenly jubilation of the saints, to taste their joy.

The saints are not a small caste of chosen souls, but an innumerable crowd to which the liturgy urges us to raise our eyes. This multitude includes not only the officially recognized saints, but the baptized of every epoch and nation who sought to carry out the divine will faithfully and lovingly. We are unacquainted with the faces and even the names of many of them, but with the eyes of faith we see them shine in God's firmament like glorious stars.

Today, the Church is celebrating her dignity as "Mother of the Saints, an Image of the Eternal City" (A. Manzoni), and displays her beauty as the immaculate Bride of Christ, source and model of all holiness. She certainly does not lack contentious or even rebellious children, but it is in the saints that she recognizes her characteristic features and precisely in them savors her deepest joy.

In the first reading, the author of the Book of Revelation describes them as "a great multitude which no man could number, from every nation, from all tribes and peoples and tongues" (Rev 7:9).

This people includes the saints of the Old Testament, starting with the righteous Abel and the faithful patriarch, Abraham; those of the New Testament; the numerous early Christian martyrs and the blesseds and saints of later centuries, [up] to the witnesses of Christ in this epoch of ours.

They are all brought together by the common desire to incarnate the Gospel in their lives under the impulse of the Holy Spirit, the life-giving spirit of the People of God.

Homily, Solemnity of All Saints, November 1, 2006

## Why Venerate the Saints?

"Why should our praise and glorification, or even the celebration of this solemnity, mean anything to the saints?" A famous homily of St. Bernard for All Saints' Day begins with this question. It could equally well be asked today. And the response the saint offers us is also timely:

"The saints," he says, "have no need of honor from us; neither does our devotion add the slightest thing to what is theirs.… But I tell you, when I think of them, I feel myself inflamed by a tremendous yearning" (*Disc.* 2, *Opera Omnia Cisterc.* 5, 364ff).

This, then, is the meaning of today's solemnity: looking at the shining example of the saints to reawaken within us the great longing to be like them; happy to live near God, in His light, in the great family of God's friends. Being a saint means living close to God, to live in His family. And this is the vocation of us all, vigorously reaffirmed by the Second Vatican Council and solemnly proposed today for our attention.

Homily, Solemnity of All Saints, November 1, 2006

## How Can We Become Saints?

How can we become holy friends of God? We can first give a negative answer to this question: To be a saint requires neither extraordinary actions or works, nor the possession of exceptional charisms.

Then comes the positive reply: It is necessary first of all to listen to Jesus and then to follow Him without losing heart when faced by difficulties. "If anyone serves Me," He warns us, "He must follow Me; and where I am, there shall My servant be also; if any one serves Me, the Father will honor him" (Jn 12:26).

Like the grain of wheat buried in the earth, those who trust Him and love Him sincerely accept dying to themselves. Indeed, He knows that whoever seeks to keep his life for himself loses it, and whoever gives himself, loses himself, and in this very way finds life (see Jn 12:24–25).

The Church's experience shows that every form of holiness, even if it follows different paths, always passes through the way of the Cross, the way of self-denial. The saints' biographies describe men and women who, docile to the divine plan, sometimes faced unspeakable trials and suffering, persecution and martyrdom. They persevered in their commitment.

"They … have come out of the great tribulation," we read in Revelation; "they have washed their robes and made them white in the blood of the Lamb" (Rv 7:14). Their names are written in the book of life (see Rv 20:12), and heaven is their eternal dwelling-place.

The example of the saints encourages us to follow in their same footsteps and to experience the joy of those who trust in God, for the one true cause of sorrow and unhappiness for men and women is to live far from Him.

Holiness demands a constant effort, but it is possible for everyone because, rather than a human effort, it is first and foremost a gift of God, who is thrice holy (see Is 6:3).... The Apostle John remarks: "See what love the Father has given us, that we should be called children of God; and so we are" (1 Jn 3:1).

It is God, therefore, who loved us first and made us His adoptive sons in Jesus. Everything in our lives is a gift of His love. How can we be indifferent before such a great mystery? How can we not respond to the heavenly Father's love by living as grateful children? In Christ, He gave us the gift of His entire self and calls us to a personal and profound relationship with Him.

Consequently, the more we imitate Jesus and remain united to Him, the more we enter into the mystery of His divine holiness. We discover that He loves us infinitely, and this prompts us in turn to love our brethren. Loving always entails an act of self-denial, "losing ourselves," and it is precisely this that makes us happy.

Homily, Solemnity of All Saints, November 1, 2006

## Love Reaches Beyond Death

The belief that love can reach into the afterlife, that reciprocal giving and receiving is possible, in which our affection for one another continues beyond the limits of death — this has been a fundamental conviction of Christianity throughout the ages, and it remains a source of comfort today. Who would not feel the need to convey to their departed loved ones a sign of kindness, a gesture of gratitude or even a request for pardon?

Now a further question arises: If "purgatory" is simply purification through fire in the encounter with the Lord, Judge and Savior, how can a third person intervene, even if he or she is particularly close to the other?

When we ask such a question, we should recall that no man is an island, entire of himself. Our lives are involved with one another; through innumerable interactions they are linked together. No one lives alone. No one sins alone. No one is saved alone.

The lives of others continually spill over into mine: in what I think, say, do and achieve. And conversely, my life spills over into that of others, for better and for worse. So my prayer for another is not something extraneous to that person, something external, not even after death.

In the interconnectedness of Being, my gratitude to the other — my prayer for him — can play a small part in his purification. And for that there is no need to convert earthly time into God's time: In the communion of souls, simple terrestrial time is superseded. It is never too late to touch the heart of another, nor is it ever in vain.

In this way we further clarify an important element of the Christian concept of hope. Our hope is always essentially also hope for others; only thus is it truly hope for me too.

As Christians we should never limit ourselves to asking: How can I save myself? We should also ask: What can I do in order that others may be saved and that for them too the star of hope may rise? Then I will have done my utmost for my own personal salvation as well.

ENCYCLICAL LETTER *SPE SALVI,* N. 48, NOVEMBER 30, 2007

## Remembering the Faithful Departed

After celebrating the Solemnity of All Saints, [on All Souls' Day] the Church invites us to commemorate all the faithful departed, to turn our eyes to the many faces who have gone before us and who have ended their earthly journey. So … I would like to offer a few simple thoughts on the reality of death, which for us Christians is illuminated by the resurrection of Christ, and so as to renew our faith in eternal life.…

During these days we go to the cemetery to pray for the loved ones who have left us, as it were paying a visit to show them, once more, our love, to feel them still close, remembering also, an article of the Creed: In the communion of saints there is a close bond between us who are still walking here upon the earth and those many brothers and sisters who have already entered eternity.

Human beings have always cared for their dead and sought to give them a sort of second life through attention, care, and affection. In a way, we want to preserve their experience of life; and, paradoxically, by looking at their graves, before which countless memories return, we discover how they lived, what they loved, what they feared, what they hoped for and what they hated. They are almost a mirror of their world.

Why is this so? Because, despite the fact that death is an almost forbidden subject in our society and that there is a continuous attempt to banish the thought of it from our minds, death touches each of us; it touches mankind of every age and every place. And before this mystery we all, even unconsciously, search for something to give us hope, a sign that might bring us consolation, open up some horizon, offer us a future once more. The road to death, in reality, is a way of hope, and it passes through our cemeteries, just as [it] can be read on the tombstones, fulfilling a journey marked by the hope of eternity....

The Solemnity of All Saints and the commemoration of all the faithful departed tells us that only those who can recognize a great hope in death can live a life based on hope. If we reduce man exclusively to his horizontal dimension, to that which can be perceived empirically, life itself loses its profound meaning.

Man needs eternity, for every other hope is too brief, too limited for him. Man can be explained only if there is a Love which overcomes every isolation, even that of death, in a totality which also transcends time and space. Man can be explained, he finds his deepest meaning, only if there is God.

We know that God left His distance from us and made himself close. He entered into our life and tells us: "I am the resurrection and the life; he who believes in Me, though he die, yet shall he live, and whoever lives and believes in Me shall never die" (Jn 11:25–26)....

Every Sunday in reciting the Creed, we reaffirm this truth. And in going to cemeteries to pray with affection and love for our departed, we are invited, once more, to renew with courage and with strength our faith in eternal life, indeed to live with this great hope and to bear witness to it in the world: Behind the present there is not nothing. And faith in eternal life gives to Christians the courage to love our earth ever more intensely and to work in order to build a future for it, to give it a true and sure hope.

General Audience, All Souls' Day, November 2, 2011

CHAPTER EIGHTEEN

# The Forgiveness of Sins

## "Return to Me With All Your Heart"

"Return to me with all your heart" (Joel 2:12).... We hear these words with which God invites the Jewish people to sincere and unostentatious repentance. This is not a superficial and transitory conversion, but a spiritual itinerary that deeply concerns the attitude of the conscience and implies sincere determination to reform.

The prophet draws inspiration from the plague of locusts that descended on the people, destroying their crops, to ask them for inner repentance and to rend their hearts rather than their clothing (see Joel 2:13).

In other words, it is in practice a question of adopting an attitude of authentic conversion to God — of returning to Him — recognizing His holiness, His power, His majesty.

And this conversion is possible because God is rich in mercy and great in love. His is a regenerating mercy that creates within us a pure heart, renews in our depths a firm spirit, restoring the joy of salvation (see Ps 51:14). God, in fact — as the prophet says — does not want the sinner to die, but to convert and live (see Ez 33:11).

The prophet Joel orders in the Lord's name the creation of a favorable penitential environment: The trumpet must be blown to convoke the gathering and reawaken consciences. The Lenten season proposes to us this liturgical and penitential environment: a journey of forty days in which to experience God's merciful love effectively.

Today the appeal "Return to me with all your heart" resounds for us. Today it is we who are called to convert our hearts to God, in the constant awareness that we cannot achieve conversion on our own, with our own efforts, because it is God who converts us.

Furthermore, He offers us His forgiveness, asking us to return to Him, to give us a new heart cleansed of the evil that clogs it, to enable us to share in His joy. Our world needs to be converted by God, it needs His forgiveness, His love. It needs a new heart.

HOMILY, ASH WEDNESDAY, MARCH 9, 2011

## Forgiveness Comes from the Cross

"Receive the Holy Spirit. If you forgive men's sins, they are forgiven them; if you hold them bound, they are held bound" (Jn 20:23). The Lord breathes on the disciples, giving them the Holy Spirit, His own Spirit. The breath of Jesus is the Holy Spirit....

To His breath, to the gift of the Holy Spirit, the Lord joins the power of forgiveness.... The Holy Spirit unites, breaks down barriers, leads us one to the other. The strength that opens up and overcomes Babel is the strength of forgiveness.

Jesus can grant forgiveness and the power to forgive because He himself suffered the consequences of sin and dispelled them in the flame of His love. Forgiveness comes from the Cross; He transforms the world with the love that is offered. His heart opened on the Cross is the door through which the grace of forgiveness enters into the world. And this grace alone is able to transform the world and build peace....

The Sacrament of Penance is one of the Church's precious treasures, since authentic world renewal is accomplished only through forgiveness. Nothing can improve the world if evil is not overcome.

Evil can be overcome only by forgiveness. Certainly, it must be an effective forgiveness; but only the Lord can give us this forgiveness, a forgiveness that drives away evil not only with words but truly destroys it. Only suffering can bring this about, and it has truly taken place with the suffering love of Christ, from whom we draw the power to forgive.

HOMILY, MASS OF PRIESTLY ORDINATION, PENTECOST, MAY 15, 2005

## "Be Reconciled to God"

The Apostle [Paul] invites us to remove our gaze from him and to pay attention instead to the One who sent him and to the content of the message he bears: "So we are ambassadors for Christ, God making his appeal through us. We therefore beseech you on behalf of Christ, be reconciled to God" (2 Cor 5:20).

An ambassador repeats what he has heard his Lord say and speaks with the authority and within the limits that he has been given. Anyone who serves in the office of ambassador must not draw attention to himself, but must put himself at the service of the message to be transmitted and of the one who has sent it.

This is how St. Paul acted in exercising his ministry as a preacher of the word of God and an apostle of Jesus Christ. He does not shrink from the duty he has received, but carries it out with total dedication, asking us to open ourselves to grace, to let God convert us. He writes: "Working together with Him, then, we entreat you not to accept the grace of God in vain" (2 Cor 6:1)....

St. Paul was speaking to the Christians of Corinth, but through them he intended to address all people. Indeed, all people have always needed God's grace, which illuminates minds and hearts. And the Apostle immediately insists: "Behold, now is the acceptable time; behold, now is the day of salvation" (2 Cor 6:2).

All can open themselves to God's action, to His love. With our evangelical witness we Christians must be a living message. Indeed, in many cases we are the only Gospel that men and women of today still read.

This is our responsibility, following in St. Paul's footsteps, a further reason for living Lent fully: in order to bear a witness of faith lived to a world in difficulty, in need of returning to God, in need of conversion.

HOMILY, ASH WEDNESDAY, MARCH 9, 2011

## LESSONS IN THE CONFESSIONAL

What is the pedagogical value of the sacrament of Penance for penitents? We should state beforehand that first and foremost it depends on the action of grace and on the objective effect on the soul of the member of the faithful. Of course, sacramental Reconciliation is one of the moments in which personal freedom and an awareness of self need to be expressed particularly clearly. It is perhaps also for this reason, in an epoch of relativism and of the consequent attenuated awareness of one's being, that this sacramental practice is also weakened.

Examination of conscience has an important pedagogical value. It teaches us how to look squarely at our life, to compare it with the truth of the Gospel, and to evaluate it with parameters that are not only human but are also borrowed from divine Revelation. Comparison with the Commandments, with the Beatitudes and, especially, with the precept of love, constitutes the first great "school of penance."

In our time, marked by noise, distraction and loneliness, the penitent's conversation with the confessor can be one of the few — if not the only — opportunities to be truly heard in depth.

Dear priests, do not neglect to allow enough room for the exercise of the ministry of Penance in the confessional. To be welcomed and heard is also a human sign of God's welcoming kindness to His children.

Moreover, the integral confession of sins teaches the penitent humility, recognition of his or her own frailty and, at the same time, an awareness of the need for God's forgiveness, and the trust that divine grace can transform his life. Likewise, listening to the confessor's recommendations and advice is important for judging actions, for the spiritual journey, and for the inner healing of the penitent.

Let us not forget how many conversions and how many truly holy lives began in a confessional! The acceptance of the penance and listening to the words "I absolve you from your sins" are, lastly, a true school of love and hope that guides the person to full trust in the God of Love, revealed in Jesus Christ — to responsibility and to the commitment to continuous conversion.

Dear priests, our own prior experience of divine Mercy and of being humble instruments teaches us an ever more faithful celebration of the Sacrament of Penance and profound gratitude to God who "gave us the ministry of reconciliation" (2 Cor 5:18).

Address to the 22nd Annual Course on the Internal Forum, organized by the Apostolic Penitentiary, March 25, 2011

## The Spirit Aids in Our Repentance

"For our sake he made him to be sin who knew no sin, so that in him we might become the righteousness of God" (2 Cor 5:11). Our possibility of receiving divine forgiveness depends essentially on the fact that God himself, in the person of his Son, wished to share in our human condition, but not in the corruption of sin.

The Father raised him through the power of his Holy Spirit and Jesus, the new Adam, became, as St Paul says: "a life-giving spirit" (1 Cor 15:45), the first fruits of the new creation. The same Spirit who raised Jesus from the dead can turn our hearts from hearts of stone into hearts of flesh (cf. Ezek 36:26).

We [invoke] him … in the Psalm *Miserere*: "Create in me a clean heart, O God, and put a new and right spirit within me. Cast me not away from your presence, and take not your holy Spirit from me" (Ps 51:10–11). That same God who banished our first parents from Eden, sent His own Son to this earth, devastated by sin, without sparing Him, so that we as prodigal children might return, repentant and redeemed through His mercy, to our true homeland. So may it be for all of us, for all believers, and for all those who humbly recognize their need for salvation.

Ash Wednesday Homily, February 22, 2012

CHAPTER NINETEEN

# The Resurrection of the Body

## Our Resurrection Begins in Baptism

Being baptized means being united to God. In a unique, new existence we belong to God, we are immersed in God himself....

With Baptism, with immersion in the name of God, we too are already immersed in immortal life, we are alive for ever. In other words, Baptism is a first stage in resurrection: Immersed in God, we are already immersed in the indestructible life; our resurrection begins.

*Lectio Divina,* Ecclesial Convention for the Diocese of Rome, June 11, 2012

## The Resurrected Body

Naturally, we cannot define the glorified body because it is beyond our experience. We can only note the signs that Jesus has given us to understand, at least a little, in which direction we should seek this reality.

The first sign: The tomb is empty. That is, Jesus' death did not leave His body behind to corruption. This shows us that even matter is destined for eternity, that it is truly resurrected, that it does not remain something lost. But He then assumed this matter in a new condition of life.

This is the second point: Jesus no longer dies, that is, He is beyond the laws of biology and physics because He endured this one death. Therefore there is a new condition, a different one, that we do not know but which is shown in the fact of Jesus and which is a great promise for all of us: that there is a new world, a new life, toward which we are on a journey.

Being in this condition, Jesus had the possibility of letting himself be felt, of offering His hand to His followers, of eating with them, but still of being beyond the conditions of biological life as we live it. We know that, on the one hand, He is a real man, not a ghost ... He lives a real life, but a new life that is no longer submitted to the death that is our great promise.

It is important to understand this, at least as much as we can, for the Eucharist. In the Eucharist, the Lord gives us His glorified body, not flesh to eat in a biological sense. He gives us himself, this newness that He is in our humanity, in our being as person, and it touches us within with His being so that we might let ourselves be penetrated by His presence, transformed in His presence.

It is an important point because we are thus already in contact with this new life, this new type of life, since He has entered into me, and I have gone out of myself and am extended toward a new dimension of life. I think that this aspect of the promise, of the reality that He gives himself to me and pulls me out of myself, toward on high, is the most important point. It is not about noting things that we cannot understand, but of being on a journey to the newness that always begins again anew in the Eucharist.

Interview for *In His Image* by Raio Uno, April 22, 2011

## Our Entire Being Enters Eternity

All of us today are well aware that by the term "heaven" we are not referring to somewhere in the universe, to a star or such like; no. We mean something far greater and far more difficult to define with our limited human conceptions.

With this term "heaven" we wish to say that God, the God who made himself close to us, does not abandon us in or after death, but keeps a place for us and gives us eternity. We mean that in God there is room for us.

To understand this reality a little better let us look at our own lives. We all experience that when people die they continue to exist, in a certain way, in the memory and heart of those who knew and loved them. We might say that a part of the person lives on in them, but it resembles a "shadow," because this survival in the heart of their loved ones is destined to end.

God, on the contrary, never passes away, and we all exist by virtue of His love. We exist because He loves us, because He conceived of us and called us to life. We exist in God's thoughts and in God's love. We exist in the whole of our reality, not only in our "shadow."

Our serenity, our hope, and our peace are based precisely on this: In God, in His thoughts and in His love, it is not merely a "shadow" of ourselves that survives, but rather we are preserved and ushered into eternity with the whole of our being in Him, in His Creator love.

It is His love that triumphs over death and gives us eternity; and it is this love that we call "heaven": God is so great that He also makes room for us. And Jesus the man, who at the same time is God, is the guarantee for us that [man and God] can exist and live, the one within the Other, for eternity.

This means that not only a part of each one of us will continue to exist, as it were pulled to safety, while other parts fall into ruin. On the contrary, it means that God knows and loves the whole of the human being, what we are. And God welcomes into His eternity what is developing and becoming now, in our life made up of suffering and love, of hope, joy, and sorrow. The whole of man, the whole of his life, is taken by God and, purified in Him, receives eternity.

Dear friends! I think this is a truth that should fill us with deep joy. Christianity does not proclaim merely some salvation of the soul in a vague afterlife in which all that is precious and dear to us in this world would be eliminated, but promises eternal life, "the life of the world to come." Nothing that is precious and dear to us will fall into ruin; rather, it will find fullness in God. Every hair of our head is counted, Jesus said one day (see Mt 10:30).

The definitive world will also be the fulfillment of this earth, as St. Paul says: "Creation itself will be set free from its bondage to decay and obtain the glorious liberty of the children of God" (Rom 8:21).

Then we understand that Christianity imparts a strong hope in a bright future and paves the way to the realization of this future. We are called, precisely as Christians, to build this new world, to work so that, one day, it may become the "world of God," a world that will surpass all that we ourselves have been able to build....

Let us pray the Lord that He will enable us to understand how precious in His eyes is the whole of our life. May He strengthen our faith in eternal life [and] make us people of hope who work to build a world open to God, people full of joy who can glimpse the beauty of the future world amidst the worries of daily life and in this certainty live, believe, and hope.

Homily, Solemnity of the Assumption, August 15, 2010

## Mary's Assumption, a Share in Christ's Resurrection

This then is the nucleus of our faith in the Assumption: We believe that Mary, like Christ her Son, overcame death and is already triumphant in heavenly glory, in the totality of her being, "in body and soul…."

St. Paul helps us to shed a little more light on this mystery, starting from the central event of human history and of our faith: that is, the event of Christ's resurrection, which is "the first fruits of those who have fallen asleep" (1 Cor 15:20).

Immersed in His paschal mystery, we are enabled to share in His victory over sin and death. Here lies the startling secret and key reality of the whole human saga. St. Paul tells us that we are "incorporated" in Adam, the first man and the old man, that we all possess the same human heritage to which belong suffering, death, and sin.

But every day adds something new to this reality that we can all see and live: Not only are we part of this heritage of the one human being that began with Adam, but we are also "incorporated" in the new man, in the risen Christ, and thus the life of the Resurrection is already present in us.

Therefore this first biological "incorporation" is incorporation into death. It is an incorporation that generates death. [But] the second, new, "incorporation" that is given to us in Baptism is an "incorporation" that gives life.…

St. Paul says: "For as by a man came death, by a man has come also the resurrection of the dead. For as in Adam all die, so also in Christ shall all be made alive. But each in his own order: Christ, the first fruits, then at His coming, those who belong to Christ" (1 Cor 15:21–24).

Now, what St. Paul says of all human beings, the Church in her infallible Magisterium says of Mary in a precise and clear manner: The Mother of God is so deeply integrated into Christ's mystery that at the end of her earthly life she already participates with her whole self in her Son's resurrection. She lives what we await at the end of time when the "last enemy" — death — will have been destroyed (see 1 Cor 15:26). She already lives what we proclaim in the Creed: "We look for the resurrection of the dead, and the life of the world to come."

We can then ask ourselves: What are the roots of this victory over death, wonderfully anticipated in Mary? Its roots are in the faith of the Virgin of Nazareth, as the Gospel passage … testifies (see Lk 1:39–56): a faith that is obedience to the word of God and total abandonment to the divine action and initiative, in accordance with what the Archangel announced to her.

Faith, therefore, is Mary's greatness, as Elizabeth joyfully proclaims: Mary is "blessed among women," and "blessed is the fruit of [her] womb," for she is "mother of the Lord" because she believed and lived uniquely the "first" of [these] Beatitudes, the beatitude of faith. Elizabeth confesses it in her joy and in that of her child who leaps in her womb: "And blessed is she who believed that there would be a fulfillment of what was spoken to her from the Lord" (v. 45).

Dear friends, let us not limit ourselves to admiring Mary in her destiny of glory, as a person very remote from us. No! We are called to look at all that the Lord, in His love, wanted to do for us too, for our final destiny: to live through faith in a perfect communion of love with him and hence to live truly.

Homily, Solemnity of the Assumption,
August 15, 2010

CHAPTER TWENTY

# And Life Everlasting

## We Long for Eternal Life

To eliminate death or to postpone it more or less indefinitely would place the earth and humanity in an impossible situation, and even for the individual would bring no benefit. Obviously there is a contradiction in our attitude, which points to an inner contradiction in our very existence.

On the one hand, we do not want to die; above all, those who love us do not want us to die. Yet on the other hand, neither do we want to continue living indefinitely, nor was the earth created with that in view. So what do we really want?...

In some way we want life itself, true life, untouched even by death; yet at the same time we do not know the thing towards which we feel driven. We cannot stop reaching out for it, and yet we know that all we can experience or accomplish is not what we yearn for.

This unknown "thing" is the true "hope" which drives us. At the same time the fact that it is unknown is the cause of all forms of despair and also of all efforts, whether positive or destructive, directed towards worldly authenticity and human authenticity.

The term "eternal life" is intended to give a name to this known "unknown." Inevitably it is an inadequate term that creates confusion.

"Eternal," in fact, suggests to us the idea of something interminable, and this frightens us. "Life" makes us think of the life that we know and love and do not want to lose, even though very often it brings more toil than satisfaction, so that while on the one hand we desire it, on the other hand we do not want it.

To imagine ourselves outside the temporality that imprisons us and in some way to sense that eternity is not an unending succession of days in the calendar, but something more like the supreme moment of satisfaction, in which totality embraces us and we embrace totality — this we can only attempt. It would be like plunging into the ocean of infinite love, a moment in which time — the before and after — no longer exists. We can only attempt to grasp the idea that such a moment is life in the full sense, a plunging ever anew into the vastness of being, in which we are simply overwhelmed with joy.

This is how Jesus expresses it in St. John's Gospel: "I will see you again and your hearts will rejoice, and no one will take your joy from you" (Jn 16:22). We must think along these lines if we want to understand the object of Christian hope, to understand what it is that our faith, our being with Christ, leads us to expect.

Encyclical Letter *Spe Salvi*, n. 11–12, November 30, 2007

## The Need for Purgatorial Cleansing

With death, our life-choice becomes definitive — our life stands before the judge. Our choice, which in the course of an entire life takes on a certain shape, can have a variety of forms.

There can be people who have totally destroyed their desire for truth and readiness to love, people for whom everything has become a lie, people who have lived for hatred and have suppressed all love within themselves. This is a terrifying thought, but alarming profiles of this type can be seen in certain figures of our own history. In such people all would be beyond remedy, and the destruction of good would be irrevocable: This is what we mean by the word *Hell.*

On the other hand there can be people who are utterly pure, completely permeated by God, and thus fully open to their neighbors — people for whom communion with God even now gives direction to their entire being, and whose journey towards God only brings to fulfillment what they already are.

Yet we know from experience that neither case is normal in human life. For the great majority of people — we may suppose — there remains in the depths of their being an ultimate interior openness to truth, to love, to God. In the concrete choices of life, however, it is covered over by ever new compromises with evil — much filth covers purity, but the thirst for purity remains, and it still constantly re-emerges from all that is base and remains present in the soul.

What happens to such individuals when they appear before the Judge? Will all the impurity they have amassed through life suddenly cease to matter? What else might occur?

St. Paul, in his First Letter to the Corinthians, gives us an idea of the differing impact of God's judgment according to each person's particular circumstances. He does this using images which in some way try to express the invisible, without it being possible for us to conceptualize these images — simply because we can neither see into the world beyond death nor do we have any experience of it.

Paul begins by saying that Christian life is built upon a common foundation: Jesus Christ. This foundation endures. If we have stood firm on this foundation and built our life upon it, we know that it cannot be taken away from us even in death. Then Paul continues:

"Now if any one builds on the foundation with gold, silver, precious stones, wood, hay, straw — each man's work will become manifest; for the Day will disclose it, because it will be revealed with fire, and the fire will test what sort of work each one has done. If the work which any man has built on the foundation survives, he will receive a reward. If any man's work is burned up, he will suffer loss, though he himself will be saved, but only as through fire" (1 Cor 3:12–15).

In this text, it is in any case evident that our salvation can take different forms, that some of what is built may be burned down, that in order to be saved we personally have to pass through "fire" so as to become fully open to receiving God and able to take our place at the table of the eternal marriage-feast.

ENCYCLICAL LETTER *SPE SALVI*, N. 45–46, NOVEMBER 30, 2007

## THE CLEANSING ENCOUNTER WITH CHRIST

Some recent theologians are of the opinion that the [purgatorial] fire which both burns and saves is Christ himself, the Judge and Savior. The encounter with Him is the decisive act of judgment. Before His gaze all falsehood melts away. This encounter with Him, as it burns us, transforms and frees us, allowing us to become truly ourselves.

All that we build during our lives can prove to be mere straw, pure bluster, and it collapses. Yet in the pain of this encounter, when the impurity and sickness of our lives become evident to us, there lies salvation. His gaze, the touch of His heart, heals us through an undeniably painful transformation "as through fire" (1 Cor 3:15). But it is a blessed pain, in which the holy power of His love sears through us like a flame, enabling us to become totally ourselves and thus totally of God.

In this way the interrelation between justice and grace also becomes clear: The way we live our lives is not immaterial, but our defilement does not stain us forever if we have at least continued to reach out towards Christ, towards truth and towards love. Indeed, it has already been burned away through Christ's passion.

At the moment of judgment we experience and we absorb the overwhelming power of His love over all the evil in the world and in ourselves. The pain of love becomes our salvation and our joy.

It is clear that we cannot calculate the "duration" of this transforming burning in terms of the chronological measurements of this world. The transforming "moment" of this encounter eludes earthly time-reckoning. It is the heart's time; it is the time of "passage" to communion with God in the Body of Christ.

The judgment of God is hope, both because it is justice and because it is grace. If it were merely grace, making all earthly things cease to matter, God would still owe us an answer to the question about justice — the crucial question that we ask of history and of God. If it were merely justice, in the end it could bring only fear to us all.

The incarnation of God in Christ has so closely linked the two together — judgment and grace — that justice is firmly established: We all work out our salvation "with fear and trembling" (Phil 2:12). Nevertheless, grace allows us all to hope, and to go trustfully to meet the Judge whom we know as our "advocate," or *parakletos* (see 1 Jn 2:1).

Encyclical Letter *Spe Salvi*, n. 47, November 30, 2007

CHAPTER TWENTY-ONE

# Amen

## "Amen" to God's "Yes"

The faithful "yes" of God and the trusting "amen" of believers enter into dialogue….

Our life and our journey are frequently marked by difficulty, misunderstanding, and suffering. We all know it. In a faithful relationship with the Lord, in constant, daily prayer, we too can feel tangibly the consolation that comes from God. And this strengthens our faith, because it enables us to have an actual experience of God's "yes" to man, to us, to me, in Christ. It makes us feel the fidelity of His love, which even extended to the gift of His Son on the Cross.

St. Paul says: "For the Son of God, Jesus Christ, whom we preached among you,… was not Yes and No; but in Him it is always Yes. For all the promises of God find their Yes in Him. That is why we utter the Amen through Him, to the glory of God" (2 Cor 1:19–20).

The "yes" of God is not halved, it is not somewhere between "yes" and "no," but is a sound and simple "yes." And we respond to this "yes" with our own "yes," with our "amen," and so we are sure of the "yes" of God.

General Audience, May 30, 2012

## Say "Yes" to God

The Church's "amen" is grafted onto God's faithful "yes," which resonates in every action of the liturgy. "Amen" is the answer of faith that always concludes our personal and community prayers and expresses our "yes" to God's project. [Even so,] we often respond to prayers with our "amen" out of habit, without grasping its deep meaning.

The word derives from *'aman,* which in Hebrew and Aramaic means "to make permanent," to "consolidate," and, consequently, "to be certain," "to tell the truth." If we look at Sacred Scripture we see that this "amen" is said at the end of the Psalms of blessing and praise, such as, for example, Psalm 41: "But You have upheld me because of my integrity, and set me in Your presence forever. Blessed be the Lord, the God of Israel, from everlasting to everlasting! Amen and Amen" (vv. 13–14).

Or else it expresses adherence to God at the moment when the People of Israel return full of joy from the Babylonian Exile and say their "yes," their "amen," to God and to His law. In the Book of Nehemiah it is told that, after this return, "Ezra opened the book [of the Law] in the sight of all the people; for he was above all the people; and when he opened it all the people stood. And Ezra blessed the Lord, the great God; and all the people answered, 'Amen, amen,' lifting up their hands" (Neh 8:5–6).

From the outset, therefore, the "amen" of the Jewish liturgy became the "amen" of the first Christian communities. Indeed, the book of the Christian liturgy par excellence, the Revelation to John, begins with the "amen" of the Church:

"To Him who loves us and has freed us from our sins by His blood and made us a kingdom, priests to His God and Father, to Him be glory and dominion for ever and ever. Amen" (Rev 1:5b–6). This is what it says in the first chapter of the Book of Revelation. And the same book ends with the invocation: "Amen. Come, Lord Jesus!" (Rev 22:20).

Dear friends, prayer is the encounter with a living Person to listen to and with whom to converse. It is the meeting with God that renews His unshakeable fidelity, His "yes" to man, to each one of us, to give us His consolation in the storms of life and to enable us live, united to Him, a life full of joy and goodness, which will find fulfillment in life eternal.

In our prayers we are called to say "yes" to God, to respond with this "amen" of adherence, of faithfulness to Him throughout our life. We can never achieve this faithfulness by our own efforts. It is not only the fruit of our daily striving; it comes from God and is founded on the "yes" of Christ, who said: "My food is to do the will of the Father" (see Jn 4:34).

It is into this "yes" that we must enter, into this "yes" of Christ, in adherence to God's will, in order to reach the point of saying with St. Paul that it is not we who live, but Christ himself who lives in us. Then the "amen" of our personal and community prayers will envelop and transform the whole of our life into a life of God's consolation, a life immersed in eternal and steadfast love.

General Audience, May 30, 2012

## Books by Pope Benedict XVI
### from Our Sunday Visitor

The Apostles

The Fathers
Volume I – St. Clement to St. Augustine
Volume II – St. Leo to St. Bernard

The Apostles, Illustrated

The Fathers, Illustrated
Volume I – St. Clement to St. Paulinus of Nola
Volume II – St. Augustine to St. Maximus the Confessor

Breakfast with Benedict

Questions and Answers

Saint Paul the Apostle

The Virtues

Great Teachers

Holy Women

Doctors of the Church

The Priest, A Bridge to God

The Environment

Prayer